A Smile Within a Tear and Other Fairy Stories

A SMILE WITHIN A TEAR

A Smile within a Tear

AND

Other Fairy Stories

BY

THE LADY GUENDOLEN RAMSDEN

" True, I talk of dreams,
Which are the children of an idle brain,
Begot of nothing but vain fantasy."
—ROMEO AND JULIET,
Act I., Sc. 4.

LONDON :
HUTCHINSON & CO.
34 PATERNOSTER ROW, E.C.
1897

AKW 7901

I.

𝔄 Smile within a Tear.

TOMMY had only one leg. He was nine years old, and it was four years since a large cart had driven over his leg whilst he was playing in the street. Then it was so badly hurt that it had to be cut off. It seemed to him now that it had happened a long time ago.

He did not miss it very much, except when he came out of school and saw the other boys jump up on a low wall and run along the top till they came to a lamp-post at the corner, and then swing themselves on to it, and slide down to the pavement again. Then he longed to do the same and couldn't.

However, if he had been running so fast on the top of the wall, he would never have known his dear little friend Elfie. Her real

▲

name was Mary; no one knew why she was always called Elfie. She was seven years old and had no mother, at least, she never remembered having a mother. She had lovely golden hair, and large, dark eyes, and Tommy said she was pretty. She was nearly as tall as him, but not near so strong, although she had two legs, and could run much faster than he could. She used to give him her bag of books to carry on coming out of school, and sometimes, not always, she used to walk home by his side to the street where they both lived, and repeat to him the stories her father, the old shoemaker, had told her. Tommy liked these stories very much indeed, but he said they weren't true. Elfie insisted that "some of it was true."

One day, just before the school holidays, she told him she was sure there were fairies, although she had never yet seen any, but she had heard them.

"Heard what? When?" said Tommy.

"Oh, several times. Once old Mrs. Carter

"She used to walk home by his side."   [*Page* 2

gave me a penny to fetch her a jug of milk. As I came back to Mrs. Carter's I thought I'd like a sip of the milk, and just as I put my lips to the jug, a little voice said softly, ' Don't, Elfie.' "

" Oh, but that was your conscience," said Tommy.

" Conscience? What is that ? "

" Ah, well, perhaps," said Tommy, " you're not old enough to understand—"

" Perhaps," she said thoughtfully, " perhaps it's the name of a fairy ; because father said to our neighbour one day, ' Have you no conscience, Mrs. Carter ? ' and she said, ' Conscience ! Conscience says stuff and nonsense.' Now, in stories, you know, fairies *always* say ' stuff and nonsense ' when they are displeased."

Tommy said nothing. They had come to a crossing, and there were so many carts and buses that they both had to watch for a safe moment, and couldn't think about anything else.

When they were safe on the other side,

they had forgotten what they had been talking about. Tommy asked her whether she was going with the other school children to the country the following Thursday.

"It's going to be a grand treat; I believe *I* am going," he said.

"Are you?" said Elfie. "I don't believe I'm asked, but I'll talk to father about it. I should like to go, too; wouldn't it be nice? In the real country, did you say? where the grass is as tall as me? Oh, how I should like to go!"

"I went once before; just a few weeks before I lost my leg," said Tommy. "It was very nice; we ran races, and jumped over a pole. I got a prize—a sixpenny bit; but, of course, now," he added rather seriously, "I can't."

"Poor Tommy, I wish you had two legs. I wish I could do something for you. I wish it was really, really true that there were fairies, then you might get a new leg from them. Oh, wouldn't that be funny?" —and Elfie laughed.

" Oh, Elfie," he said, " you're a dear, kind little friend, but when will you stop talking about fairies? There's no real sense in it all."

"Ah, well! Tommy, I don't think you're at all nice, and I am not little, I am as tall as you nearly; and—and—as to sense," she added, nearly crying, " well, *you* may think me silly, but father said the other day that there was more sense in my little finger than in many grown-up people's heads. Father is a very, very clever man, and has read lots and lots."

" Yes, Elfie, your father is clever, they all say, but rather queer, you know."

" Well, then, it's good to be queer, for father is very good; I know he is. Perhaps it's queer to be good."

" Please don't be cross; I did not mean to be disrespectful to your father, and you know we never quarrel, you and I?"

" No, we never quarrel; but I wish you could understand about fairies—father does— and it makes one much more comfortable, somehow, and it *is* a *little* true, you know, only not quite."

"Good-bye, little fairy, then," he said, and flung the string of her bag over her head. "There you are at your door."

She stood on the step of the house a minute, and watched him hopping as fast as he could with his crutch. When he turned the corner of the yard where he lived, he waved his cap in the air, and she waved her hand in return. Then she burst into her father's room, and flung her arms round him.

"Still at work, father!" she exclaimed; "isn't it nearly tea-time?"

"Yes, child, you can get it ready; but I must finish putting a patch on this boot, for old David wants it to wear to-night."

Elfie was a handy little girl, and soon spread the table with a cloth, and set the tea things on it. They had cold tea, because it was very hot weather, and they had bread and butter, and a very little bacon.

Presently, when they sat down, she said:

"Father, what does 'queer' mean?"

"Did any one call you a queer, little girl?" he asked her, smiling.

"Only you, father, as a joke, when I asked you to explain about the stars the other night, don't you remember, and old David was listening, too, and he shook his head so"—she shook hers to show him—"and he said, 'Well, well, it's a queer world.'"

"'Queer' only means peculiar, not common; and sometimes people say a thing is queer when they can't understand it."

"Ah! now I know, father, why people call *you* queer! It is because they don't always understand what you mean. Then they don't know you, of course, as well as I do! Now, you are not the least queer to me; you always explain everything so clearly, I think. But what did David mean when he said the world was queer? Did he mean it was different from the other worlds, the stars? or did he mean he couldn't understand?"

"I think he was puzzled and could not

understand.   There are things so beautiful and wonderful, that even grown-up people can't understand."

"Oh, yes, the stars, for instance. I suppose unless one could fly and see them, one could not understand them. Would it not be nice to fly, father? Oh, father!" she interrupted herself, "Tommy is going to the country on Thursday for the school treat. Shall I be able to go?"

"I've heard nothing about it, dear; but if it's for the board school I fancy they won't leave you out."

On Thursday morning, Miss Burton, one of the teachers, came into the passage, and called at the adjoining house:

"Annie! Annie! are you ready?"

Elfie knew Annie was a little girl who lived with her granny, Mrs. Carter, on the top storey.

"Shall I run up and fetch her?"

Miss Burton nodded, and tapping her hand impatiently on the banister at the foot of the stairs, she said:

"Tell her to be quick, for the van is nearly full, and we shall start in ten minutes."

Elfie had scarcely reached the second landing before Annie came down in a smart, new, blue cotton frock, and a white hat with blue cornflowers on it.

"I'm sorry to be late; it was granny's fault." The two girls came down together. "I'm so sorry, Elfie, you're not coming," she whispered; "but Miss Burton says the treat is only for Sunday-school children."

Miss Burton overheard these words, and smiled kindly at Elfie.

"Perhaps there'll be a treat for all the board school before the summer is over, and then you'll come. It's a pity your father never sends you to Sunday-school."

"Father says he does not belong to the church, that is why," she answered, blushing.

She followed Miss Burton and Annie at some distance; she wanted to see the van. When she got near to Tommy's house he was standing ready, dressed, leaning on his crutch.

"Elfie!" he said, "I don't think I'll go after all. I think I'll stay and talk to you; only let's go and see the van start."

"Would you stay away from the treat for my sake, Tommy?" and she opened her large eyes still more in astonishment. "I don't think I could do as much for you."

He answered: "But, then, you're only a girl, and—and—not so old as me. I—I—don't so much care for treats, perhaps," he said meditatively, as he hobbled along.

The next turn brought them close to the vans. There were three; two were quite full; the third was filling fast. The horses had ribbons, and there were four little flags, one to each corner of the vans.

The children were shouting, and laughing, and talking, and making such a noise that Elfie could hardly hear her own voice, as she said to Tommy:

"I know I am not so kind as you, but, dear Tommy, I'd rather you went, and then you'll tell me all about it to-morrow. It would make me miserable to think you stayed away for my sake. Think of the grass, and flowers, and birds, you'll see. Why, you'll have enough to talk about for a week! Do, dear Tommy, go; and you'll see I sha'n't mind one bit being left behind! Father and I are 'queer,' and we don't belong to the church; but I can be brave, too, Tommy, although I'm only a girl."

Tommy still hesitated, then he said:

"It's true I'd see a lot if I went, and I'd tell you everything I see, and I'll bring you back half my flowers; of course the other half will be for mother. If you're sure, quite sure, you won't cry, I think, after all, I should like to go very much."

"Oh, I sha'n't cry," she answered, and she pressed her lips rather tight together, as she stood with her hands behind her back, and stared up at the van, and at the chimney-pots of the houses on the other side of the yard, and at the blue sky beyond. Tommy was the last to get in. He looked at her wistfully, and nodded; but she

seemed to be looking over his head. There
was a cracking of whips, and shouting, and
cheering, and then the vans drove off. Out
of the yard they went, and away down the
crowded street. The rumbling of its wheels
could no longer be heard, and all became
quite still in the yard.

Elfie still stood immovable, looking at
some white clouds in the sky. Presently a
quantity of sparrows came close to her feet.
She looked down and watched them as
they quarrelled over a piece of a bun one
of the children had dropped. There was
one little sparrow that seemed to be hurt,
for it could not fly very well, and the others
kept pecking it whenever it tried to get one
little crumb for itself. "Poor little bird!"
said Elfie out loud, and she felt in her
pocket if, by chance, there was a crumb.
Yes! there were a few, so she very, very
gently turned her pocket inside out, to let
them fall to the ground. The poor little
sparrow presently came nearer and nearer,
as Elfie stood still, and picked them all up;

and then it twittered to thank her, and flew away. The others were still too busy quarrelling to notice what had occurred.

She then turned to go home. Only a few children passed her, and some stood at the doors of their houses. She supposed they, too, had not been invited. Perhaps because they did not belong to the Sunday-school. She thought the day would seem very long, but it must come to an end sometime; and late in the evening—perhaps when she was in bed—the vans would return. To-morrow Tommy would be sure to come and see her.

It was only half-past seven o'clock, but she had got up earlier than usual to see the vans. Now it was breakfast time, so she hurried in to put it all ready for her father. She always did this, only her father would not let her touch the kettle, as it was too heavy for her.

She felt rather sad, and not very hungry. She had hoped, and hoped to the last, that perhaps she should still be invited to join the treat. Miss Burton always had said Elfie was a good little girl, much more diligent than Annie. But then Annie attended the Sunday - school very regularly— that was the difference.

Why had she never been to Sunday-school? Her father always taught her himself on Sunday mornings. She could sing the same hymns as Annie, for they sometimes sang together, and Mrs. Carter said they both sang sweetly.

When breakfast was ready, and after her father had poured out the coffee, she said :

" Father, why don't you send me to the Sunday-school ? "

He paused a moment before answering, and then he said :

" Because I don't agree with some things they teach in the Church of England. When you are old enough to understand, you shall choose whether you shall belong to the Church, or what denomination you like best. As long as you are a good little girl—I mean a good Christian, Elfie—I shall not mind if you don't

agree with me in everything. I am sorry
you have missed this treat to-day; but I
am going to work very hard, and then perhaps on Saturday I can take you to the
Park."

"Oh, that will be very nice!" she said;
but she thought it would not be so nice as
going for the whole day to the country with
the children, and she felt a large lump coming in her throat, and she wished to cry,
and she couldn't eat much. Her father
kissed her, and then he went to the window,
and began to work again.

She tried not to cry, and began washing
up the cups and things before putting them
by. Whilst she was doing this, she said to
herself: "When I am older I shall choose
which nomination—no, to which nominative
case—I shall belong. But then I am sure
I shall agree with father, as we always do
understand each other. Or, supposing I *did*
choose to belong to the Church, why, then
I shall be too old to care for the Sunday-
school treat. Oh! how I wish I was sitting

in the fresh green grass, and picking flowers with Tommy!"

She felt very unhappy; but she had told Tommy she should not cry, so she tried to keep down her tears. But she was not attending to what she was doing, and, instead of emptying the slop-basin into the pail of dirty water, she took the sugar-basin and emptied that by mistake. The noise of the lumps falling in, made her suddenly see what she was doing. So she went to her father and told him :

" I am so, so sorry, father; and I'll do without sugar for two weeks, to make up for all I've wasted."

But he only smiled rather sadly, and said :

" Never mind the sugar, little Elfie; but I'm afraid it means you're very unhappy, for you never were clumsy like this before. I'm so sorry, my poor little girl," and he drew her into his arms, and kissed her again.

She murmured : " You are so dear and kind, I'm not so very unhappy!" but she felt the lump in her throat almost choking her, so she slipped back to the other side of the room, and finished tidying everything away.

After that she took out some piece of work to hem, and sat down on a low stool, and leant against the old horsehair sofa. She sat with her back to the window, because she did not want her father to see she was crying. The tears welled up now : she could not prevent them. She could not see to work, and she could not find her needle. Large hot tears kept coming and rolling down her cheeks, till they dropped on to one of her hands, and then the tears felt cold.

One tear fell just on the top of another, till they seemed to be one large tear in the palm of her hand. This large tear grew larger and larger; and the sun was shining over the top of her head on to the tear, and it glistened like crystal.

Still the tear grew larger and larger, and it seemed to her that she was shrinking and

B

getting smaller and smaller. It was a curi-
ous sort of feeling, but not unpleasant. She
felt happier, and no fresh tears came, only
that big tear had now grown so large, and
she felt so small, that she wondered how such
a very, very little girl could have cried such
a big tear, for it seemed to fill the room.

It had the appearance now of a very pretty
bubble, with many colours in it. She looked
at it very attentively, and saw on one side
of it a little knob.

"Oh, I see," she said, "it's not a tear!
It's a large air ball, and that knob is where
the string is tied!"

She put out her hand to feel for the
string, for she could not see it. But to
her surprise she felt the knob turn, like
the handle of a door! She had scarcely
touched it when it flew open, inwards, and
she saw about four crystal steps leading
into a lovely garden.

"Oh," she said, "I see now; it's some
fairy garden, and as the door is open, they
can't mind my walking in."

So she stepped very carefully down the glass steps; they felt rather slippery, but she managed it all right. Then all the ground was covered with soft green moss, and all sorts of flowers were growing here and there. There was no path, and she felt a little puzzled at first which way to go, until she perceived in the distance some trees. She then walked towards them.

"It's lucky," she said to herself, "the moss is deliciously soft to walk upon, for I see now I've not got my shoes and stockings on! However, I can't go back and fetch them now. If I do meet a fairy she won't mind, because I shall tell her that it's only because I am 'queer,' and not that I'm disrespectful."

When she came to the trees, she saw they were overhanging a lovely little stream of clear water; so clear, that though it was rather deep, she could see all sorts of different coloured pebbles at the bottom, and some pink and green weeds all fluttering and bending with the stream. These weeds seemed to be almost dragged away, roots and all, by the water, so strong was the current here.

Presently she saw there was a very funny old man sitting on the opposite bank. He was dressed very oddly, in green velvet, just the colour of the moss, that is why she had not observed him before. By his side he had a large basket full of fish, and he kept lifting them out, one by one, and gently dropping them into the stream. The fish were very lively the instant they touched the water, and swam away, some up and some down the stream.

"Now, this is very queer," she thought, "I mean very peculiar! I often have seen people fishing, and taking fish out of the water, but this man puts them in!"

She hid her feet in the longest tuft of moss she could find, because she did not want the funny man to see she had naked feet, and then she called out to him:

"Do you mind telling me why you do

that? what kind of fish are they? are they good to eat?"

"You're a stranger, I can see!" He grinned, and showed a row of very black teeth.

"I wonder if he ate too much sugar when he was little, and whether it made his teeth like that?" she thought.

"These fish, my little stranger, are what we call here *human soles*, I'm throwing them into this stream called 'the Church.'"

"Oh!" she said, "and do they belong to the Sunday-school?"

"I don't know," he answered, "they settle all that for themselves. Once in the stream they can go up or down, or do what they like; I don't care, it's not my business. I can only speak for an hour, so I'd rather talk about something more amusing."

"Only for an hour! Why?" she asked, surprised.

"Because after that my teeth begin to ache for four hours, and I can't open my mouth."

"Oh, I am very sorry for you; can nothing be done to do you good?" she asked.

"No, thank you, nothing at present. I ate too many sugar plums and lolly-pops once upon a time. I spent all my pocket-money in buying them, and so now for a time I am punished in this way. I can only talk for an hour, every four hours."

"Perhaps then we had better talk of something else, as you have so short a time."

She watched him putting in the fish for a few minutes, and then she smiled and said :

"This is a beautiful country, but I don't see many people. Isn't it rather lonely?"

"Yes, it's beautiful of course here, little stranger, and it's full of people, only of quite a different kind than you are. You will understand it all presently when you're older."

"I'm so tired of being told that, would you mind—" she said gently, "would you mind not saying that again, because it will take me years and years to grow up."

"Ha, ha, ha, ha! not *here*, little stranger! Here you will grow older in a few hours. But what I meant is that when you get older (I will only just mention it once more), when you are a few hours older, you will understand that you're not lonely, for the trees, and birds, and flowers, and water, and stones, all can speak when you have learnt their language ; besides, of course, there are the inhabitants."

"Are you an inhabitant ?"

"Oh, no, I'm only the servant, the 'odd man' who is employed to do odd jobs."

"Will you be so kind as to tell me where I am ? I mean the name of this place ?"

"It's called—oh ! oh! my teeth !" and he shook his head.

Elfie at once understood he could no longer talk. He had emptied the basket of fish by this time, and sat with his head bent over his knees. Elfie was very sorry, but she felt she could do nothing for him, besides there was the little stream between them. Being a little London child, she did not know how to jump, although it was quite a narrow steam, and easy to get over.

She sat down on the moss and looked up into the trees. There she saw a crow eating a cream cheese, and in a minute she had quite forgotten the odd man.

"That is very funny, Mr. Crow; you and I have met before. I know you quite well!"

"Caw, caw," he said, but he did not drop the cheese, for he spoke with his beak shut; but she managed to catch his words. "Are you the little girl who can't repeat the fable about me and the fox without making a mistake?"

"You should not say that, Mr. Crow; you should name yourself last. 'The fox and me,' you mean? Yes, I know it quite well. Shall I repeat it now?"

"Oh, no, for Crow's sake, don't, unless

you can repeat it in French. Caw!
Caw!"

"Is that French? Caw? Caw?"

"Oh, what an ignoramus you— There,
you have made me drop it. Caw, caw."

The cream cheese fell to her feet.

She picked it up and placed it on the
highest branch she could reach, which was
not very high. The crow smiled and flew
down, and carried it up again to where he
was before.

"Merci! That's French for 'thank you.'
I was afraid you would have eaten it," he
said.

"That," she said proudly, "would not
have been honourable."

The crow now spoke with his beak full,
and so it was very indistinct, but she understood him to say that there was another
acquaintance standing behind her.

She turned sharply round and saw a frog,
very smartly dressed, walking on his hind
legs, holding an umbrella. He looked so
proud of himself, and at the same time so

ridiculous, she nearly laughed out loud. The frog was far too much occupied with rolling up his umbrella very tight to notice Elfie's titter of laughter.

When he had buttoned it, he put out his paw and said :

" Delighted to see you! Everybody knows me, though I can't say I care to know everybody ; but I am delighted to make your acquaintance, Miss—Miss—?"

" I am not Miss anything! I am just Elfie ; and I have met you before, of course, many times, Sir—Sir Anthony?"

"You are labouring under some erroneous idea. I am the frog who would a-wooing go, madam."

" Oh, of course! I was making some stupid mistake ; but now I remember. I have often puzzled over your life, Mr. Frog, and now I am so glad to have met you face to face, for you will explain it all to me."

" Pray, be seated," he said, and waved his paw.

His manners were so peculiar, and his

words so long, that Elfie could hardly prevent herself from laughing again.   Luckily,
he did not observe it.

" I daresay, madam, I can throw some
light upon the matter, if you will be explicit
in describing what has proved to be your
stumbling-block.   Although I must caution
you that there are occasions ' where ignorance is bliss, 'tis—'   You know, dear
madam ?   You know ? "

He sat down very near her.   She thought
his manners rather familiar, and so she moved
a little farther away on the moss, and said
rather coldly :

" I don't like being called 'dear,' unless
it is by a relation or—or a very great friend."

" I beg your pardon, madam.   It is a trick
I've got since a-wooing I did go—o! ho!
ho!" and he began to sing.

Here the crow gave a ghastly laugh, such
as can't be described, because to hear a
crow's laugh is very rare.   But it startled
Elfie very much, and she began to wish
she could go away.   She regretted now

having greeted the frog so warmly. He seemed to her rather vulgar, and not like a gentleman. However, she resolved to ask him some questions, and after that she would walk away and leave him.

" Well, Mr. Frog, there are three things that puzzle me. The first is, Who is Sir Anthony Rowley, who keeps say-ing ' Heigho !' every minute in your story ? Is he a human being ? or another frog ? or a roley-poley pudding ? or what ? You see, I know your wife, the mouse—"

" Yes, Mistress Mouse," the frog in-terrupted her.

" Yes, Mistress Mouse, and the lily-white duck that—that— I don't like to finish for fear of hurting your feelings."

" Pray, don't consider them at all, if I can be of any assistance in disentangling this Gordian knot ? "

" I mean the duck that swallowed you up. I say I know them and you by the pictures ; but I never saw Sir Anthony, although I've often looked for him. Also what puzzles me is, that if you were gobbled up, how is it that you are still here? And one more question, Are you any relation to that frog who wished to be as big as the ox?"

"Sir Anthony, dear madam—I beg your pardon, *madam*—is as much a myth as I am a reality. In my opinion, he is an unnecessary appendage to an otherwise moral, and, at the same time, poetic, tale."

Here the crow groaned with suppressed laughter, and Elfie began to wonder if the frog was quite sober.

He continued, "Then, as to the duck, read '*tried* to gobble him up'; that is the new translation. As to that other frog, he was a Socialist, who wished everybody to be equal. He was no relation of mine, and is 'bust up,' and I hope all of his persuasion will end thus."

At this the crow said, "Hear, hear, hear!" and was quite serious again.

Elfie thought it was a good moment to say good-bye, so she put out her hand.

"Thank you," she said, "for answering all my questions."

"Not at all; it has been a pleasure to converse with one so cultivated and intellectual as you are, madam. I may add Mistress Mouse was—I mean is—a widow, and I am still wooing her. I am on my way there now. May I ask for the pleasure of your company?"

Elfie looked up in the tree, expecting that dreadful laugh again, but the crow had flown away.

"No, thank you, Mr. Frog, not to-day," she said, and curtseyed. "I must walk on now."

She felt ashamed when she got up, remembering she had no shoes or stockings on. She blushed, and looked to see if her feet showed very much in the moss; but she was surprised to see she had silk stockings on, and they were *blue*.

"When people are learned," she thought, "they are called 'blue stockings,' but I should not have thought I had learnt so much as all that, although one certainly does get to know things very quickly here. I wonder what 'myth' means. I did not quite understand all that frog told me. Myth, moth. No, it can't have anything to do with a moth. Myth? Myth—if I repeat a word like that, it sometimes explains itself." So she walked on, looking on the ground, and thinking over the word. At last she stopped and exclaimed, " Mythical! That means not quite true, not quite real. I must ask father by and by to tell me what it means exactly."

She had walked a little way up the stream when she came to a bridge over the brook. It was made of china, blue and white willow pattern.

" That is nice," she said; " I shall now cross the Church stream, and I think I'd better walk down on the other side and see if the odd man is suffering with toothache still. It would be kind, just to show him I had not forgotten him."

She was just in the middle of the bridge when her feet seemed to touch some spring, and first she heard a click and then a buzz, just like a musical box. She clung to the side of the bridge, and then the tune burst forth of " Onward, Christian Soldiers."

She was startled, but when she heard the tune she said, " I know that," and she sang the words with the music. When it was finished there was a click, and it stopped. " Thank you," she said, because it seemed a fairy bridge and could understand.

She stood in the middle again, and pressed her foot.

" Can you please play 'There's room for little Mary'? or if it is too long, please will you play 'Knocking, knocking'?"

There came a great buzz and a click, and then nothing more.

" Oh, I beg your pardon, I forgot; perhaps you prefer 'Ancient and Modern,' and they are very pretty, too. Please play 'There's a crown for little children,' I can sing that."

There was a buzz, and then the music began again, and Elfie sang it with all her

heart. When it was quite finished there
came a little tiny voice, but, oh, so tiny,
like the voice of a mouse, and it said:

"That was pretty; you sing very
nicely."

"Thank you, you're very kind to say that,"
said Elfie, as she crossed the bridge.

She found so many streams on the other
side that she could not get very far. After
stepping over one or two very small ones,
she met an old woman in a red cloak and
hood.

Elfie smiled, and put out her hand, and
asked her if she was Cinderella's godmother.

"No," the old woman answered rather
sadly, "only Mother Hubbard, at your ser-
vice," and she curtseyed in an old-fashioned
way.

Elfie said: "Oh, but where, then, is your
dog?"

The old woman answered: "He's at home.
I heard there was a little girl here, and I
thought as I'm very fond of children I should
like to talk to you."

c

"Thank you, that is kind," Elfie said; "but do I still look like a child? I feel ever so much older since I came in here, and the odd man said a few hours would make me older."

"Yes, in knowledge, child, but not in years."

"Oh, I am glad of that, because it's so nice to be young—I mean, to be a child," she added, because she did not want to vex Mother Hubbard by reminding her she was old.

"I daresay it is nice to be young. I never was young. I always was Old Mother Hubbard," she added rather sadly.

"Dear Mrs. Hubbard," said Elfie, purposely leaving out the word "old," "may I take hold of your hand and walk about with you? I want to understand so many things here that seem—peculiar."

"Yes, I will take hold of your hand, because we must carefully pick our way over these streams."

"I've been wondering why there are so

many, and so near together. Why don't
they all run in one big stream?"

"Because the fishes in them are different,
and they would not agree if they were all
together."

"I was told the one I crossed by the bridge
is called the Church—Church of England?
Have the others names, too?"

"Yes, there's the Quaker stream, and the
Wesleyan, and the Methodist, and the Presby-
terian, you see, there," and she pointed to
the different brooks. "The fish are obliged
to be kept separate up here, as they would
quarrel; but when they get down in the great
river below, they forget all their differences."

"I suppose because it's larger, and there
is more room?" asked Elfie.

"Oh, it is large enough, for it is endless."

"Really? Endless? I like endless things
so very much—when they are pleasant, of
course, I mean. Don't you, Mrs. Hubbard?
I hate an end; the end of a story, or the
end of a holiday, because then comes good-
bye, and that is the word so often makes

one feel uncomfortable—an end-of-everything-happy-a-crying sort of feeling."

"Yes, child, but old people are nearer the endless, and yet—and yet—" and Mother Hubbard wiped her eyes.

Elfie thought perhaps the old woman had some real, great sorrow. Many grown-up people have had sorrows, she knew. Then, to change the conversation, she said:

"Which are the best fish? I mean, in which stream are the best fish put?"

"There are good and bad in each, but if they once can get into the large river they become perfect. In each stream there are fish that miss the way, and get lost in dark, muddy water, under weeds or rocks."

"What a pity," said Elfie, and she walked on silently for a few minutes, then she asked:

"What is the name of the large, endless river?"

"It's the river of Love."

"Oh, can you take me to it now? I should so much like to see it. The only river I've seen is the Thames."

"We are walking towards it now. I will take you by a short cut when we've crossed all these streams. They go winding about a long way round."

Mother Hubbard walked very fast now. Some of the brooks they stepped over, and others had planks and bridges; but there was no such pretty or musical bridge again as the first. At last they came to a wood, and here was a road. Many old friends of Elfie's met her. The cat and his fiddle came first with his company. She saw the cow, and rather wished to ask her how she managed to jump over the moon. But she did not like to stop Mother Hubbard, who seemed to be in a hurry. After that she saw Jack and Jill, and little Bo-peep, and Mary and her little lamb, and many many, others. They all nodded to her, and seemed pleased to see her. She heard the bells of London town, too, and that surprised her, for she saw no houses or churches — nothing but beautiful trees overhead. The bells seemed invisible, and, what was still more surprising to Elfie, they did not say the old story, beginning with, "You owe me ten shillings," but they rang a peal as for a wedding, and the words were : "Tommy and Elfie will marry. Tom-my and El-fie will mar-ry each other!" and the old Bell of Bow kept repeating, "and re-pent it at leisure — at leisure."

"How very odd, Mrs. Hubbard! They are singing about Tommy and me! How do they know my name?"

"The bells are great gossips; they always know everything."

"Hark! Mrs. Hubbard, what the bell with the two high notes is saying!" And the words were : "Tom-my has but one leg," and then backwards, "Leg one but has my Tom."

"Oh, pay no attention to them, child. They don't mean it unkindly."

"But it's quite true that Tommy has only one leg! Do you know any fairy who could give him another?"

"Yes, child, I know of one ; but I don't

advise you to go near her, for though she might give Tommy a new leg, it would be full of evil consequences."

"Oh, would it really?" and Elfie thought a little while, then said, "What should you do if some one you loved had only one leg?"

"I should love him still more, and try to think of all the pleasures that I could procure for him, in spite of his one leg."

"How tiresome those bells are. They keep repeating what we say, and what they have already said, all mixed up. Can't you stop them, Mrs. Hubbard? It is not respectful."

The bells rang out louder than before:

"Elfie—Tommy—one leg—marry—repent —leisure."

"Elfie repent—Tommy repent—leg repent —leisure repent."

Elfie looked as if she was going to cry, but soon such deafening laughter and cheering and vulgar singing was heard, that Elfie forgot all about the bells. She saw "Old King

Cole" coming along. His nose was much bigger and more red than any picture of him she had ever seen.

Mother Hubbard pulled her quickly out of the road.

"There are all those noisy people," she said. "Come away quickly," and she tapped at a large oak tree. A door opened in its trunk. In they slipped, and shut it again instantly. Elfie peeped through a little hole, and she could see King Cole walking along, followed by his fiddlers singing: "And a merry, merry soul was he, he, he, was he, he, he!" He was very big, and touched the branches of the trees with his head. Whenever his nose touched a leaf, it fizzed up and was burnt; and all the gnats and flies in the air flew to it, as they do towards a candle, and dropped down burned.

"Come," said Mother Hubbard, "that's not a pretty sight. Follow me if you want to see the river to-day. It's getting late."

She stamped her foot once, and struck a match, lit a little lantern hanging to the wall, and looked on the ground. She waited a minute, then stamped again, and a door opened at their feet, and Elfie saw steps.

"Isn't it rather dark? Is there no gas?"

"Gas? stuff and nonsense! Who ever heard of gas in this country? Follow me," and she stepped down the stairs, holding the lamp on the top of her head, so that Elfie might see better.

Elfie felt a little—just a little—frightened; but she had gained much confidence by the words, "stuff and nonsense," because she saw at once that Mother Hubbard was a fairy after all. No one but a fairy ever answers in that way. Sometimes, she knew, they added "pooh" to "stuff and nonsense."

She stepped carefully down after her, but the steps were very deep and large. She had to keep putting both feet on one step, down, down, down, straight down first, and then round and round, till at last they reached a lovely grotto. The sun was shining in, and Mother Hubbard blew out her lantern.

"Now, here we are close to the river; but

there are a few difficulties to be got over by yourself. I must not help you any more. You will see the river in a minute."

She pointed to the opening of the grotto, but the light was so bright Elfie could see nothing in that direction; so she looked back into the grotto, to where Mother Hubbard stood.

"Oh, how pretty it all is! Why, this grotto is made all of shells and coral! Oh! oh! how lovely! But don't leave me yet!" she said, taking hold of Mother Hubbard's hand. "It surely has not come to an end? not an end?"

"No, child; only an end for the present."

Elfie watched her while she said this very slowly. Mother Hubbard stood about two yards off, near the wall of the grotto, just in the rays of the sun that were slanting in. Mother Hubbard's face had become quite young. Her red cloak had vanished, and she looked like a beautiful fairy—all glittering. She smiled very kindly, and looked quite amused as Elfie stared at her. Such a sweet

and beautiful smile she had! Then gradually
—gradually she faded away into the sunbeam,
and there was nothing of Mother Hubbard
left except the endless recollection of her kind
smile.

Elfie had never seen anything so beautiful. There was still the sunbeam, and she
knew if she followed it she would find the
river, so she did not feel unhappy. She
repeated to herself, "only for the present,
I shall see her again!" then she wondered
what the "difficulties" would be that she
would have to overcome.

Her eyes had now got used to the light,
and she could see all sorts of shells in the
walls of the grotto, and white and pink
coral. There were pearls, too, in some of
the shells. But although it was all so lovely,
yet she never felt inclined to pick out a
shell or anything. She thought it might
all vanish if she touched it.

She slowly walked out into the outer air,
and then—and then—she saw and felt her
difficulties! She had no longer blue stock-

ings; her feet were again naked, and all the ground was crawling and creeping with toads, and frogs, and serpents, and beetles. They did not hurt her, only they were so fat, and slimy, and cold, and wet, and slippery, and clammy, and nasty, and horrid, and there was no room to walk without treading on some.

Elfie shouted out, "Oh, how disgusting!"

Then they all lifted their heads, and said:

"But we are your fellow-creatures all the same, and it's kind of us not to bite you, for you are a remarkably heavy young woman!"

In a minute she felt sorry.

"I was a—a little surprised, and I was told this was the only way to the river of Love, and I would much rather not tread on you, but there seems no room here."

She tried not to tread heavily, and to pick out the largest toads, because she thought they looked the most solid.

One large beetle put up his head, and said:

"You have not acknowledged us as your fellow-creatures. You're too proud, are you?"

"Oh, no, I'm not proud; but I must speak the truth. I have never considered you as my fellow-creatures."

"Well," said a serpent, "are you not a creature?"

"Yes, of course," she said, trying to get past without touching him, but she slipped on to his tail. "I beg your pardon," she said.

"You need not, for I rather like your treading on me," said the serpent. "People generally run away from me."

"But to return to the subject," said the beetle, "you say you're a creature, and so are we, so we must be your *fellow-creatures*, don't you see?"

"Yes, I see now you are my fellow-creatures, only not those I like best."

"Still we are? we are? we are?" they asked, all round.

"Yes," said Elfie, "you are."

Then they all laughed.

"We thought you would not acknowledge us, but you have!" and they all flew up into the air, and became different coloured birds.

The ground was now nice clean sand, and she saw, close to her feet, the river—very, very broad, and in the middle there was a little boat that seemed to be hurrying towards her. It was in the shape of a large shell; the sails were made of rose leaves, and in it were a quantity of little children as pretty as angels. When they came near the shore they beckoned to her to come. She ran into the water, for it was quite shallow, and she climbed into the boat very easily.

"We are so glad to see you, Elfie, and we will now have great fun!"

They all kissed her, and she felt very happy to have so many companions to play with, and she was just going to tell them so when she sneezed, "A—kêtchum! A—A kêtchum!" and she woke up, and found it was all a dream! . . .

" They beckoned to her to come." [*Page* 46.

Her father had kissed her, and now said :

"What a long, long sleep you've had! Why, do you know you were asleep at dinner-time, and it's now tea-time!"

But Elfie felt so puzzled and confused she only rubbed her eyes, and said, very sleepily :

"Was I asleep? I suppose I must have been dreaming? I was just going to go down the river in a boat, and, father, it was so very, very real!"

"Well, Elfie," he said, "you shall tell me all about it by and by; but now you must be very hungry, and see, I've got such a nice fish here, fried!" and he lifted the steaming cover off the dish.

She was very hungry, and soon wide awake enough to eat a very good tea.

"When will the vans come back, do you think, father? Shall I still be up."

"I should think at half-past eight, so you can wait to see them come home. I'll go with you."

Elfie bustled about after tea, and put by everything right, and made no mistakes this time. He father had soon finished his work, and they both went out, walking down into the street.

It was not very amusing; they knew all the shops so well; but they stood a long time at Elfie's favourite shop, which was full of rabbits, and mice, and birds. There was a beautiful white cockatoo, but *he* could not talk, she knew, and the grey parrot, who could talk, was cross or ill, and would not say a word.

There was also a shop full of prints, and as her father had read so much, he knew all about them, and explained the stories of the pictures to her. Some time after that, as they were approaching the yard on their way home, they heard the vans coming. The children were cheering, but they had been too tired to do so until just as they came near their homes.

There were many parents waiting to welcome their children back again. Tommy's mother was too busy to be there; she was a widow, and had to work very hard to keep Tommy and herself in food and clothes, but she could hear the vans from her window, and she was very glad when she heard them come home.

Tommy got down at last, and Elfie slipped into the crowd to get near to him.

"Well, Tommy, did you enjoy yourself?" she asked him; but Tommy looked so unhappy, and only answered :

"Oh, where are my flowers? my flowers? I fell asleep, and I'm afraid I must have dropped them. Oh, dear! oh, dear! oh, Elfie! they *were* so pretty, and I'd got such a nice bunch for you!" and Tommy began to cry.

Elfie had never seen Tommy cry; he had always told her it was only little girls that cried.

"Dear, dear Tommy!" she said, "never mind the flowers; come and tell me all you saw."

"But I *do* mind!" and he tried to climb

D

into the van again to look for them, and his eyes were so full of tears he could not see to find the steps. Elfie was crying, too, because she never had seen Tommy look so dreadfully unhappy.

There were a quantity of children all round, some talking and laughing, and others quarrelling. "Who's got my hat?" said one. "I know I had that pretty stone in my pocket; you took it, Jane!" said another; and so on.

Suddenly the vicar's kind voice was heard.

"Here, children, let me pass—I want to speak to Tommy. Tommy, my boy! are you there?"

But Tommy was crying so, he could not speak; so Elfie answered:

"Here is Tommy; but, sir, he's lost his flowers!"

"No, he hasn't," said the vicar; "it's all right, my little man, I've got them! I saw you dropped them on the road when I followed in the next van. I picked them up and took care of them; look, they are quite fresh."

Tommy smiled through his tears, "Oh, thank you!" and put out both his hands to take them, resting his arm on his crutch. He did not speak, but pulled the piece of grass that tied them, and Elfie saw there were two separate bunches. He gave her one.

"Oh, Tommy, how kind you are; they *are* pretty; buttercups and daisies, and some cornflowers! or poppies! What are those blue ones?"

"I don't know; they grew near some corn in a field."

They walked together a few steps to his house. She carried both nosegays for him, but she kept smelling her own and smiling with pleasure.

Her father remained behind talking to the vicar, for her father had read so many books that the vicar said it was a pleasure to talk to him, although they did not agree on some matters. They were talking about some news in the papers, and they seemed to be of one mind about that.

Tommy told Elfie to put her flowers in water, and in the morning to cut a little tiny piece off each stalk, and give them fresh water again. He said the daisies were drooping, but would recover soon. Then he said his mother would be expecting him, and he left Elfie on the steps and went in. After what seemed a long time to Elfie, her father came towards her, and they both hurried home.

Of course Elfie put the flowers in water, and next morning did all that Tommy had told her to do. She found there was one little fern with a root. Her father planted it in a small box in earth, and it grew very well for many months.

Nothing particular happened for the next few years. Both the children were getting high up in the school, and Tommy wrote the best handwriting of any boy in his class. He also could draw very well, and during the holidays Elfie would tell him a part of the wonderful dream she'd once had. She could only remember some of it, but she described it so well, that he said he would draw pictures of the people in the wonderful country.

They both used to laugh over these drawings, especially the one of " Old King Cole," for Tommy would make him look like old David the greengrocer, and he was a teetotaller, and never drank anything but water; but that was their joke.

When Tommy grew up he became clerk and accountant in the large print shop, that Elfie and her father had often admired. His mother died when he was still a boy.

Elfie became a nurse in an hospital for children. She was not only very clever at nursing, but all the children were very fond of listening to her fairy stories, for she knew so many and told them so well that some of the little children said she helped them with her stories to forget their pain. Sometimes, when they had been extra brave and good, she would go to her cupboard and fetch the bundle of pictures drawn by Tommy. There was one little boy in the hospital who had lost his leg, and who was very fond of " Nurse Elfie." He was particularly pleased to look at these pictures, and wondered if he should ever grow up to be as clever as Tommy.

When Elfie was five-and-twenty she married Tommy, and it was only then that she told him about the bells in her dream. He laughed very much. Tommy said he had always loved Elfie, but he wouldn't ask her to marry him until he had made money enough to provide for her, so that she need not work any more after they were married. He went on working, and earned a very good salary. They lived very happily together, but Tommy was never a very strong man, and Elfie had many anxieties about him, as he was often ill.

Her father became ill when he was very old. Elfie had many anxieties about him, too, until he died.

She had three little children, and they

were a great comfort and happiness to their father and mother; but whilst they were little they were a great trouble, because they had the measles, the chicken-pox, the whooping-cough, and the mumps, and all that sort of thing. When they weren't ill they scalded themselves, or burnt themselves, or cut themselves, or bruised themselves just a little. But they all loved each other and their parents very much.

When Elfie was an old woman she said to Tommy that though there had come many anxieties, and some sorrows, to them during their lives, yet there had always been a smile within each tear.

And now if you would like to know some of the stories that she used to tell the children in the hospital, and later on to her own children, you have only to turn this leaf, and you will find some of those they liked best.

II.

"Maid or Mouse?"

THERE was once upon a time a little girl
called Jane, who was maid-of-all-work in a
London lodging. The landlady, Mrs. Hardstick, had engaged her as a "general servant,"
so she always spoke of her as "the general."
On the ground floor there lived two old
maids, ladies who had once been well off,
—"decayed gentlewomen," Mrs. Hardstick
called them. Certainly everything about them
looked worn, and shabby, and decayed,
except their hearts, which were good, and
kind, and warm, as in their youth; but Mrs.
Hardstick knew nothing about hearts, because she had never had one. But "the
general" knew that when she did anything
for these gentlewomen it was always a pleasure and not like work, for they spoke so

kindly to her; even when she had not cleaned
anything properly, or when she had forgotten
something, they never scolded her, only they
looked sorry then.   They were the only
people who called her "Jane," and did not
speak of her in the third person.

When she first came she was very awkward.
Once she spilt some cinders all over the
carpet.   Another time, in shaking crumbs
out of their linen table-cloth, she flicked it
into the fire, and burnt a hole in it.   Another
time she broke a cup that had belonged
to the decayed gentlewomen's mother.   She
had been vexed with herself for being so
stupid, and all the more so because, instead
of scolding her, Miss Angelica, the elder of
the two sisters, had only exclaimed, "Dear,
dear, what a pity! but you've always told
us the truth, and so, Jane, we won't say
anything more about it."   Afterwards, she
saw Miss Angelica mending the cup with
diamond cement, and tears were in her eyes,
whilst Miss Amelia, the younger sister, was
darning the linen cloth, and seemed to have

great · difficulty in threading her needle.
When Jane saw what trouble her awkward-
ness had caused these old ladies, she cried
until her eyes were very red, and then resolved to be much more careful in future.

On the second floor were the best rooms,
but they were not really grand at all. They
were dirty, and the furniture was very old,
but there was more light. Mrs. Hardstick
called them the "best rooms," and asked
the best price for them. Sometimes they
were unlet and locked up ; but, now when this
story begins, they happened to be inhabited
by a foreign gentleman and his wife. Jane
never could pronounce their name—" Mr.
and Mrs. Fedlaviska." Mrs. Hardstick called
them "the foreigners" or "the Fiddlewhiskys." They were both very hot tem-
pered and cross. They both practised on
two different instruments when at home.
They were out a great part of the day—
giving music lessons, they said. In the morning and evening they wore dressing-gowns,
and Mrs. Fiddlewhisky, when not playing

her instrument, would sit and copy out her
husband's compositions, while he sat at the
piano and practised, to keep his fingers
supple. When his wife practised her music,
he'd sit with his feet at the fire, smoking
a pipe, and passing both his hands through
his long hair, thinking, or grumbling, or
reading some foreign newspaper.

He told Jane she must never be heard,
as he had very sensitive nerves, and that
noise drove him mad. She was also never
to be seen, because he only liked beautiful
things to look at, and she was so ugly.
Mrs. Fiddlewhisky might have been pretty
once, but now she was fat, old, untidy,
and dirty, just like their surroundings.

Jane wondered what beautiful things he
ever had to look at. Sometimes, through the
half-opened door, she used to see him looking in the cracked looking-glass over the
chimney-piece, and perhaps he thought his
reflection beautiful. Jane liked his music
very much, when she had time to listen for
a few minutes on the stairs; but Mrs.

Fiddlewhisky's instrument Jane neither liked
nor understood.   It was not a piano, not
a violin, not a harp, and not a banjo; it
was not anything Jane had ever seen or
heard before; but then she worked very
hard, and had no time to see or hear much
beyond what went on in Mrs. Hardstick's
house.   Mrs. Fiddlewhisky had broken the
bell in their room, so when she wanted
anything she popped her head out of the
door and called for Jane, "Cheneral,
cheneral!"   Then she'd send her for things
she wanted, and take them from Jane's
hands at the door, because her husband
could not stand seeing the general's red hair,
and poor little, ugly, freckled face. Jane did
not mind—she knew she was ugly; but she
wished Mrs. Fiddlewhisky would not want
so many things, and make her run up and
down stairs so much.   In the morning it
would be "Cheneral, bring zome hot vater
for de professor!" "Cheneral, de professor
vants zie milk for his café." Hardly had
she brought it, when she had to run down

again for a saucepan, "I mõst boil de milk myzelf; you English know noting." They never seemed to have a real meal; but then they may have gone to some eating-house for that. All that Jane knew they had was vinegar, and oil, and milk, and onions, and cabbages, and eggs, and coffee, and cheese, and bacon. Mrs. Fiddlewhisky cooked it all herself, in some foreign way, and Mrs. Hardstick said "made a foreign smell with it, too ! "

On the storey over that was a pale man, Mr. Leek, a printer, who slept all day and worked all night. Jane had to make his bed, and light his fire at six in the morning, just before he returned.

Then came two attics over his room under the roof, one large and one small. In the large one Mrs. Hardstick and two children slept, and the small one was Jane's room. It was more like a large cupboard with a window than a room. Sometimes the children cried and made a noise in the night; then Jane did not sleep many hours, neither did Mrs. Hardstick. On these occasions the children and their mother would be very cross next day, and all the little general did would be wrong. She had to help to dress the children every morning after having lit the fires for Mr. Leek, the Fiddlewhiskys, the gentlewomen, and in the kitchen. The cleaning up in the pantry and scullery she always did at night before going to bed. On Saturdays Mrs. Hardstick helped her to sweep and clean out most of the rooms. Some were only cleaned once a month, when a woman came to help. Saturdays were the days Jane disliked most, because it was run, run, and work, work, all day, and late into the night, too!

Sunday she took the children out. One she pushed in a perambulator, and the other she led by the hand. If the children were good these walks were rather nice. There was a small garden near, which had been a churchyard; here Jane used to like to sit th the children. There were three or four trees and some benches. A little grass was trying to grow among the old tombstones, which had been removed and put all together in one corner. It was called a garden, but there never were any flowers to be seen, except a very few crocuses in the spring. The little Hardsticks were sickly children, and often the one in the perambulator cried, and the one that was led refused to go where Jane wished, and dragged till her arm ached. When this happened she felt very cross, worried, and unhappy.

However, one particular Saturday something very odd occurred that changed her life completely. She had been working harder than usual. She had scrubbed the whole of the staircase from the top to the bottom, besides all her other work. Unfortunately, Mr. Fiddlewhisky slipped on a little piece of soap Jane had left on the stairs, and he fell down three or four steps! He only bruised his leg a very little, but there was such a hullaballoo as never was! Mrs.

Fiddlewhisky rushed out in a red flannel
dressing-gown with all her hair down. She
screamed, and complained to Mrs. Hardstick
that "de cheneral vould cause de professor's death zome day!" Mrs. Hardstick
boxed Jane's ears till she felt quite dizzy,
and told her she was "not worth her salt!"

Later, Mr. Fiddlewhisky walked out of the
house quite lame, and swearing in a "foreign
way." He went to give some music lessons,
and when he came back he'd forgotten to
limp, and ran up two steps at a time to tell
Mrs. Fiddlewhisky some good news he had
heard.

In the meantime, Jane had been in disgrace
all day all about the piece of soap "that
might have killed the lodger of the best
room." "The professor might have fallen
on his head; then he would have had
a concussion of the brain." "He might
have broken his leg," and "he might have
broken his arm," and "he might never have
been able to play the piano again." All
these "might - have - beens" and reproaches

were thrown in Jane's teeth until the evening.

She worked on until twelve o'clock, when, at last, she was allowed to go to bed. After saying her prayers, she lay down on her little bed, but tried in vain to sleep. Her head ached, and her back ached, and she cried, and turned about on her bed, groaning and murmuring:

"I am the most miserable little girl in the world! Everybody is so unkind. Everybody says I am so stupid, and good for nothing, and I feel *so, so, so* tired, I wish I could die."

Presently she heard a little scratching in the wall behind her bed.

"Ah, that's mice! Now, they are going to make a noise, and how can I sleep?"

The scratching grew louder and louder.

"I hope it isn't a rat," she thought.

She then struck a match, very gently, for fear that Mrs. Hardstick should hear her, and lit the candle. No, it was a mouse coming out of a little hole in the wall

E

near her bed. Now, she was not frightened
of a mouse, and she was so glad to see
that it was not a rat that she felt rather
pleased than otherwise.

She whispered: "Well, come in, Miss
Mouse. There are some little crumbs in
my shoe—how they got there I don't know
—but you're welcome to eat them, only,
please, don't make a noise. I am very
tired, and I want to sleep."

To her great astonishment, the mouse
answered in a still smaller whisper:

"Thanks, but I am not come for that.
I think I heard you say you wished you
were dead?"

"Yes, I did say it; but it was naughty.
I did not really mean it. Are you a fairy?
If so, please don't hurt me. I don't want
to die at all, only my head aches, and I'm
very, very tired and unhappy."

"Exactly," said the mouse; "that's just
what I thought. Now, I am not a common
every-day mouse, and I'm tired of this sort
of life. Would you like to be me, Jane,

just for a day or two, so that you might
curl yourself up and rest? If so, I should
like very much to be you for a time, for—
for reasons of my own, which would take too
long to explain."

"Let me think," said Jane. "Would I
like to be you? Ye—es, I think I should,
for a little time. I should like to run into
that hole and hide myself, and *rest*, and
rest."

"Well," said the mouse, "then, the only
thing for you to understand is, that once a
mouse from this moment, you must remain
a mouse until one o'clock on Monday. That
is four-and-twenty hours. Is that a bar-
gain?"

"Yes, I agree, if you promise me that
I can become myself again on Monday at
one o'clock in the night."

"I promise. But, quick! shut your eyes!"
Then there was a silence for an instant,
and Mrs. Hardstick's clock struck one. Before Jane had time to think anything at all,
the mouse laughed, and said, "Look!"

She opened her eyes, and there in bed, in a night-gown, she saw an ugly, little red-haired girl, just what she knew she was herself, but with strange, large black eyes like beads, with no light in them, and, as it appeared to her, full of mischief. She then looked down to where she stood her-self, just at the foot of the bed, and found she had changed into a little grey mouse; but had she seen herself in a looking-glass, she would have observed that her blue eyes were full of light and soul. There she was, sitting up on her hind legs, and rubbing her front paws together. She tried to talk, but her voice was very small and weak.

" Now, remember," said the mouse, " you're a mouse. Don't sit and look at me like that. You must not use your front paws like hands. You must run on all fours; also, don't let the tail hang down, as if it did not belong to you ; you must give it a curl, and twist it about. You'll find it very convenient."

" Shall I ?" answered Jane, and she turned

"There in bed . . . she saw an ugly little red-hair girl."   [*Page* 68.

round to look. "I daresay I shall get used to it, but at present it feels extremely awkward. I don't think I quite like feeling so very, very small; and I am sure I sha'n't like running on all fours; but I suppose I must, when I have to run away into your hole."

"Of course you must, or you won't get down. You will find that hole leads to a great many passages. First, go straight, then take the third turn to the right, the next to the left, then the tenth turn to the right again, and there you are."

"Thank you; but I don't feel like a mouse yet; it may come in time. At present I still feel like Jane, and am very tired."

"No headache, I hope?" said the mouse.

"No; my head is so small, I suppose it can't ache, which is a comfort. Could you open the bed, and let me lie down for the rest of the night?"

"Yes; certainly. I feel still very mousish, very wide awake, and very hungry. Go to sleep, and I'll just run down to the pantry."

The mouse jumped out of bed, and, forgetting she was a girl, tried to run in the hole. Of course she banged her head against the wall.

"Oh, how stupid of me; I forgot I am too big. Well, here's a go! I want something to eat. I am very hungry, and crumbs are no good; I must have a slice of something nice and large."

Now Mrs. Hardstick popped her night-capped head suddenly in at the door, and said :

"What on earth is the general doing? Sitting on the floor in her night-gown, talking to herself, and burning my candle! Go to bed this minute, or I'll—"

The mouse looked up saucily and answered her :

"I was disturbed by a mouse, but I'll blow out the candle." She jumped up. "Puff," and all was dark.

Mrs. Hardstick muttered something, and went to bed again.

" She'll beat you if you don't mind," said Jane, peeping her tiny head out of the bed-clothes. " Do be quiet till seven in the morning. If you will only let me sleep, I can tell you all about the work you'll have to do to-morrow, Sunday."

" To-day, you mean."

" Yes, yes. Oh, *do* let me rest ! " And in two minutes Jane was fast asleep.

Not so the mouse, whose eyes seemed used to the dark. She peeped through the key-hole, and waited till Mrs. Hardstick began to snore ; then she gently, very gently, opened the door, and crept on all fours very softly through Mrs. Hardstick's room to the door into the passage. Then she rose and tried to open the door, but it was locked. She turned the key round. It squeaked in the lock. There was a " click," and the mouse feared Mrs. Hardstick would wake. No. All was silent, except her snoring, and one of the children turned in its bed. The mouse waited, and then gently, gently crept out, and closed the door after her. Now,

then, for a lark! Scamper, scamper she
went downstairs.

"Oh, bother these hands, they are so
inconvenient for running down stairs! And
bother the night-gown, it is so in my way!"

At last she came down, and into the
pantry. Now for some food! But Jane
had put by everything tidily into the cupboard
and locked it, and given the key to Mrs.
Hardstick. There were a few scraps left in
a plate in the corner, certainly, but when
she smelt it, she said:

"Only dry bread! They have been cleaning something with it. It might do for a
common every-day mouse, but not for me.
Oh, no!" She thought a little minute.
"No good trying the gentlewomen's room.
Old maids, they are! I know, when I was
a mouse, it was never worth while trying
to find anything there. Why, they'd starve
a mouse even; and I say I want a big slice
of something—something nice. What's the
good of being a girl, with hands that can open
cupboards, if I can't find something to eat?"

She remembered the best room.

"Ah," she thought, "their cupboard's open, and those foreigners have chocolate, great lumps of chocolate! Oh, how jolly I feel, I feel!" she went on to herself, as she crept up to Mr. and Mrs. Fiddle-whisky's door. "I say, I feel as if I could eat a whole pound of chocolate, and perhaps a large slice of cake, too!" She began to turn the handle. "Oh, bother; what a mousish bother! It's locked. What do they want to lock themselves up for? Old humbugging musical folks! Won't I play them some trick before I'm many hours older. Won't I just!"

Then she remembered the printer.

"Out all night, just the man to suit a mouse with a girl's appetite; no, I mean a girl with a mouse's appetite; no, I don't quite mean that, for I feel as hungry as a hundred mice; but I mean I cannot alter my mousey nature, because I happen, for the present, to have a girl's body! Awkward thing this body is! Now, if I was as small as a mouse I could have run in under the foreigners' door! Yes, but then how could I get the glass cupboard open where they keep the chocolate ? Oh, I know well enough where it is, only it's no use, as I can't get in."

When she got to the printer's room she looked into all the cupboards.

"Four lumps of sugar ! Well, that's better than nothing, but it wasn't worth all the time I've wasted."

She peeped into the inkstand, into the coal-scuttle, just out of curiosity. The clock on the mantel-piece struck five o'clock.

"What a time I've been!" she said to herself; "soon I must go to Jane, and get her to explain my duties to me. I suppose I must do some of the work. I can't shirk it all, but I won't do more than I can possibly help, and I'll try to eat as many goodies as I can get hold of. It is certainly all rather amusing!" and she gave a jump into the air just like a mouse, but she came down with such a plump that she shook the room a little.

Then from behind the bed-curtain came the
sound of something between a yawn and a
groan, and a sleepy voice muttered :

"It's a comfort it's Sunday to-day. Oh,
dear," and then another yawn.

"Good gracious," said the mouse, "the
printer's there all the time! I did not know
it was Sunday. Oh, how dreadful if he's
seen me!"

She crept out quietly on all fours, and left
the door open. She did not dare to close it
for fear of making a noise, and waking the
printer quite up.

She now hurried back to Jane, so softly,
so like a mouse, that Mrs. Hardstick never
heard her.

Jane was awake.

"It's very funny, but I feel quite rested.
I suppose my body is too small to want very
much sleep."

"Oh, I daresay," said the mouse ; "but
now tell me what they'll expect me to do."

"Well, Miss Mouse," said Jane, "first—"

"Don't call me 'mouse,' it makes such a

confusion," the mouse interrupted. "You can remain 'Jane,' but I will be 'the general.'"

"Well, general, first you'll have to—but what *have* you done to my night-gown? Why, I do believe you've been crawling in the cinders and soot, on all fours. Oh, how dirty, and it was clean on last night. Oh, dear, I shall have to sleep in my chemise for the rest of the month."

"Jane, now, don't bother. While you're a mouse you don't want clothes; you look quite neat." She spoke sharply, so Jane said nothing. "Go on, now, and tell me my duties."

"Well, first you must dress, and put on all those things on that chair." But as the mouse began to dress in what she saw first, "Oh, no!" exclaimed Jane, "put on the dress *last*, and last of all the apron."

She was obliged to explain everything to the mouse, for she was very ignorant about every-day things; she said so herself. Then Jane told her what fires to light, and about the gentlewomen's breakfast.

"You must be very particular about their things, they are so kind, and real ladies, you know."

"Oh, yes, real mouse starvers, I know. Well?"

Then Jane told her all the other things, including washing the children, and taking them out for a walk.

In return the mouse said:

"Remember there are many passages when you're in my hole; but I'll repeat: First, go straight, then take the third turn to the right, the next to the left, then the tenth turn to the right again, and there you are!"

"And where's 'there'?" asked Jane.

"Why, of course, the store-room in the next house, where there's excellent rice, flour, and sometimes sugar."

"Oh, thanks; but I'd like to explore, and see how mice amuse themselves, and how they make their passages, and all that sort of thing. By the by, will the other mice hurt me?"

"Oh, no; they'll see at once you're not an every-day mouse. You have blue eyes. They will be rather afraid of you. You might find it useful to say this one word, if you can remember it : Tarraputchicattiwalli, Tarraputchicattiwalli !" the mouse repeated.

"What does it mean?" asked Jane. "It sounds like swearing. If it's that, even in mouse language, I should not like it."

"No, it's nothing bad. I object to swearing, too. It's just a word that means many different things. It will make the other mice friendly at once. It depends on the tone of voice. If you say it quickly, and in a cheery voice, it is equal to your proverb, 'When the cat's away, the mice play.'"

"Oh! that will be rather amusing," said Jane.

"Yes; but remember it's only amusing *if the cat is really* away! In the neighbouring houses there are cats. Remember, they will think you're an every-day mouse, and gobble you up in no time! Do be careful for your own sake, and for my sake! I'm

not sure I should like to remain a girl all
my life; and if you die before one o'clock
Monday morning, there I am, you know,
'the general' all my life."

"Oh, I'm not afraid of a cat! Mind you
don't make the Fiddlewhiskys too angry, or
they might kill you, especially the professor.
He has an enormously strong wrist, and he
might kill you by mistake, if he gave you
a box on the ear. I don't want to remain
a little mouse more than a day. So you'd
better be careful."

" Never fear, I can manage those foreigners.
But you must remember you're the mouse,
and, if you see a cat, run into the first hole
you find."

" Tarraputchicattiwalli !" laughed Jane, and
such a funny little mouse's laugh it was.

Mrs. Hardstick called out : " Is the general
still talking to herself? Lazy girl ! get up
this minute !"

Away rushed Jane into the hole, and the
general went to Mrs. Hardstick, and ran
through her room, and downstairs, to light

all the fires, except Mr. Leek's fire.   He
was never disturbed on Sunday till the afternoon.

The fires were all laid, and the work was
lighter on Sundays. The general was clever
in soon catching up the proper way of walking and using her hands; only she was very
easily startled, and the least thing seemed to
make her jump.

The little Hardsticks were waiting to be
washed, while their mother unlocked the
cupboards in the pantry. The general looked
wistfully at the cheese she saw there, but
had to go up to attend to the children. She
did not like water, so she only sponged them
over, and quickly dried them, which seemed
to satisfy the children very well, for they hated
water, too. She had great difficulty in dress-
ing them, and putting their arms into the
right arm-holes, and not into the leg-holes,
which was what she tried to do at first, only
Alexander, the eldest, held up his leg indig-
nantly, and said:

"Ou silly general! my 'ittle leg goes in there!"

After they were dressed, she put the youngest on a shawl on the floor, and gave it a reel of cotton to play with.

" It's safe so," she thought. " It can't fall any lower, if it's on the floor, so it won't hurt itself. It's head is awfully tender—looks as if it might crack, like the empty shell of an egg."

In the meantime Alexander had gone to a low cupboard, and pulled out an old toy—a woolly cat, and began to pet it.

" Pussy! Pussy! dear old pussy!"

In an instant the general gave a shriek, and ran up the bed-post. There she was, sitting on the top of Mrs. Hardstick's four-post bed, when this person entered the next minute.

" Who screamed? I hope the general didn't slap either of you?"

" Oh, no, mum, but it was the sight of that cat; I am a little nervous this morning."

" Where are you?" said Mrs. Hardstick, looking all round the room.

F

"Up dar!" said Alexander, pointing to the top of the bed.

"Bless the cat!" said Mrs. Hardstick, "whatever are you doing up there?"

"Oh! please, please, Mrs. Hardstick, don't bless him! I am so frightened I can't come down."

"Frightened at the cat? Why, it isn't alive even, it's a toy! Surely you've seen it hundreds of times before? Whatever makes you so queer this morning? Come down directly. There's Mrs. Fiddlewhisky been bawling your name for the last five minutes."

"Is it only an imitation cat?" said the general, as she slid down, and stared at Alexander and the toy. "I've never seen one before."

"How black ou eyes look!" said Alexander. "Ou have got dreadful black eyes this morning. I don't like ou look at me like that!"

The general said nothing; she was still trembling with fright.

" Well, be off! will you? The foreigners are holloaing for their breakfast," said Mrs. Hardstick, angrily.

The general did as she was told, and ran up and down the staircase half a dozen times, as quickly as Jane would have done. Only so softly that the professor did not observe her, and once she came right into the room, and put down the jug of milk close to him. Mrs. Fiddlewhisky was poking the fire, and did not notice her either. Before leaving the room she made a grab at the chocolate in the open cupboard, and ran down with two large pieces. She then jumped up on the dresser in the kitchen, and ate it up in two or three minutes, whilst she sat there with her legs curled up under her. No one saw her. All her movements were very quick, now that she had got more used to her body. It was only now and then, when she forgot she was a girl, that she astonished the lodgers by her mousish ways. For instance, when the gentlewomen told her she had forgotten

to put the sugar with the other things on
the breakfast-table, she was in such a hurry
to fetch it, that she popped her head into
the cupboard, and brought out two or three
lumps with her teeth, and laid them on the
cloth before Miss Amelia's cup. The
gentlewomen were first speechless with surprise, and then exclaimed:

"Jane! how shocking! What manners!
How dirty! I can't possibly eat that sugar."

"Oh, I beg your pardon," and the
general laughed, then pocketed the lumps.
"I was forgetting who I was," she added,
still giggling, as she fetched the sugar
basin.

Miss Amelia and her elder sister ex-
changed glances. When Jane left the room
to fetch some clean plates, Miss Angelica
said:

"Dear love! that child seems very
strange this morning."

"Yes," said Miss Amelia, "I fear, dear
heart, she is hysterical. Did you hear her
laugh when we rebuked her?"

Miss Angelica shook her head, and lifted up her mittened hand.

"Indeed, indeed, Amelia, I fear since yesterday, when Mrs. Hardstick boxed the child's ears, she has not been herself."

"She is too young for all the work there is to be done here."

"Did you notice how very dark, almost black, her eyes looked when she laughed?"

"Yes, love! Now you mention it, that must have struck me when she came into the room the first time! I could not think why she seemed so altered. Surely her eyes are of a palish blue generally?"

"Hush, here she comes," said Miss Angelica.

As the general entered, Mrs. Fiddle-whisky's voice could be heard, "Cheneral! cheneral, vill you not côme ôp? De professor has de headache, and he vants—" but what he "vanted" was not heard, for the general closed the door quickly as she brought in the plates.

"The professor's knob aches! I guess

that old hoarse god-mother's throat will ache if she keeps on holloaing like that!" she exclaimed.

" Jane, your language is not becoming; you really must restrain your tongue!" said Miss Angelica.

" I beg pardon, I feel rather upset this morning, and—and strange in my new— Oh, I say, you won't like this plate!" she exclaimed, looking at the one she was just going to give Miss Amelia. "Something is smeared on it. Allow me!" and quick as lightning she licked the plate, and, turning her head to look over her shoulder, she murmured to herself, " I forgot. I do miss my tail to wipe up things with," she then lifted the end of her dress up, and wiped the plate clean with it, before presenting it again to Miss Amelia.

Both the gentlewomen got up.

"This is too bad! Jane, we desire you will leave the room instantly!"

" Why, what have I done ? I've cleaned the plate for you. I thought you were real gentlewomen, and liked clean things!"

"Ough," said Miss Angelica. "You dirty girl, dirty, dirty girl; and after all the pains Miss Amelia and I have taken in teaching you! Go away, we will wash the plates ourselves."

"I don't feel hungry, love," said her sister. "I'll wash the plates for you. Really, I can't eat anything after seeing Jane lick the plate, lick, actually li— Ough!" and Miss Amelia shuddered.

"Cheneral! cheneral!" was heard, as the general slunk out of the room, looking ashamed of herself.

"Well, it's all very queer, I can't understand their ways. What's tidy as a mouse seems dirty as a girl! I almost wish I was myself again."

She ran up and down after that for the professor and his wife till twelve o'clock, and then it was time to walk with the children.

The general started all right, pushing the perambulator with one hand, and holding Alexander by the other. She did not know

which way to go, but Alexander seemed inclined to walk towards a square, so she
went round the square once, and then down
a long street of houses. It was rather dull.
However, all went well; the children seemed
quiet and good. She told the eldest a story
of how a mouse once managed to escape out
of a trap, which delighted the child. When
they had walked nearly an hour she thought
it might be nearly dinner time, and she
turned back towards home.

On the way, when about half-a-mile from
Mrs. Hardstick's house, she was just thinking how successful she'd been, not even
having seen a cat, or anything to frighten
her. Then, to her horror, out of a house
they had passed, there bounced two large
dogs, jumping and barking in front of their
master, waiting to see which way he meant
to go. The man stood looking at his watch,
and seemed undecided.

The general started and trembled.

" Oh, dear, what horrid, large dogs ! "
Alexander began to cry when he saw how

frightened she was.   " Let's run," she said,
and away she rushed along the street.

Alexander's hat flew off, and rolled along
the gutter.   The baby's cushion fell out, and
its head went wobble, wobble, rattle, rattle,
against the perambulator.   Faster and faster
the general flew, for she heard the dogs
were coming the same way.   Alexander felt
as if his arm would be dragged off, and he
was so out of breath he could not scream,
but the baby yelled enough for both.   Luckily
it had a warm, wadded hood which protected
its head from being really hurt.

The general now heard the dogs close to
her.   Mad with fright, she left the perambulator, let go Alexander's hand, and, overcome by her mousish nature, she looked
about for a hole to escape in.   There happened to be one of those round holes in the
pavement where they shoot down coals.   At
a glance she saw it was not quite closed.
With a desperate effort, forcing her fingers
under the iron cover, she managed to turn
it over, and immediately flung herself in head

foremost. Luckily for her, and for Jane,
her dress caught in a nail or something,
and she hung head downwards, but did not
fall down into the coal cellar, or she would
most certainly have been killed. She
screamed out something in mouse language
that no one could understand, but the man
with the dogs had seen what had happened.
He knelt down on the pavement, put in his
hand, and pulled out first one little leg and
boot, and then the other. Then he stood
up, and gave a great tug, and up came the
general.

But oh! what a sight she was! Her face
was covered with black dust, her frock all
dirty and torn, her red hair all hanging over
her eyes, and one of her hands was bleeding.

The dogs, in the meantime, were both
lying quietly on the pavement watching their
master. The children both were squalling
a few yards off. A policeman had come up,
and was helping too. The general stood
trembling and jabbering to herself in mouse
language.

" The dogs are as quiet as lambs, my girl. Why are you so frightened? See! there they are, quite good. They only bark just when they first come out."

But the general only stared, and said nothing.

" Very careless to leave this hole open," said the policeman. " But I wonder how she fell head foremost?"

" It's very lucky," said the man, " the silly child was not killed."

At last the general gasped out: " Hold the dogs, and I'll go home with the children," and she began pushing the perambulator.

The children were now only whimpering. The policeman carried Alexander, and walked home by her side, while the man led his Newfoundland dogs in the opposite direction.

The policeman told Mrs. Hardstick the general had fallen through a coal hole whilst running away from some dogs. He also told her to wind a rag round the general's finger that was bleeding, which she did, and sewed it on. After the policeman had gone, she scolded the general for coming home like a chimney-sweep. She sent her to wash, and told her she'd find some dinner in the kitchen screen, which was more than she deserved.

The general did not wash, but ate some cheese and rice pudding she found, which suited her taste better than the hash of meat put ready for her. Then she felt awfully tired, and so, as she saw the fire was not too hot, she jumped into the kitchen screen, curled herself up in a corner, just like a mouse, and soon slept there, next to a pile of plates.

In the afternoon Mrs. Fiddlewhisky screamed in vain for the "cheneral." The professor was ill in bed, she said. Mrs. Hardstick could not find her, and had to do all the work herself; but even she was not allowed to enter the professor's room. Of course everybody was very angry; but it was no use, for the general was nowhere to be found. The gentlewomen were very sorry, and said they were sure "Jane must be off her head," and reproached themselves for having scolded her in the morning. "She must have run away, poor child, and what will become of her? Perhaps she's drowned herself! You had better let the police know." But Mrs. Hardstick, though she looked worried and anxious, said, "She was not going to have the police to create a scandal in her house." She attended to the gentlewomen herself, and carried up the coals and gruel to the Fiddlewhiskys' door. And now we will leave them for the present, and follow Jane in her wanderings.

When first Jane entered the hole, she was struck with the nasty mousey smell and the darkness. These two things were very disagreeable to her. Also she longed to walk on her hind legs, but when she tried to do this she hit her head, so she had to submit to her altered condition, and run along on all fours in the passages, and only stand up when she emerged into some room. Then if anyone had noticed her, they would have laughed, for she looked so funny walking thus, holding her head up proudly, and carrying her tail in her left front paw. She explored many passages. They all led to some stores or pantry, or where there was food to be found. She would not touch anything that did not belong to her; only when at last she felt hungry, she found her way into Mrs. Hardstick's kitchen (that was the time the general was out of doors) and ate a few little clean crumbs she found, and a tiny little piece of meat the gentlewomen had left in their plates. " If they knew all," she said to herself, " they would not mind my eating what they have left." There was nothing very interesting in the mice passages. She said " Tarraputchicattiwalli " once or twice when she met a mouse, but they fled from her. Very likely she said it with an accent that sounded strange to mice.

Once in wandering up, instead of down, she found herself under the roof, and here she was very much amused to find the mice having a sort of parliament. At least, she fancied it was, because the mice were all

"'Let me look at the tip of your tail,' said the mouse."   [*Page* 95.

sitting in rows, and listening to one mouse who seemed to be making a speech. When he had done, another mouse rose on the opposite side and spoke. She could not understand the language, but it seemed very serious and business-like. One mouse seemed to be the king. He was larger, and sat in the middle. Jane longed to be able to understand. She stood up in a dark corner at a little distance. Presently rather a large mouse she had not noticed standing near her, addressed her in English.

" You are not really a mouse," it said ; " I can see it in your eyes. You seem to have a large soul."

" Yes," said Jane quietly, for she was surprised at nothing now. " I'm a girl ; I've only changed bodies for a time."

"Let me look at the tip of your tail, please."

" Certainly," said Jane, and she handed it to her.

"Ah," said the mouse, " I thought so! You've got my daughter's body. I'm the president's wife. There, that's him," and she pointed to the biggest mouse. "Our daughter," she went on, with a sigh, "never can settle down contentedly with us. A fairy gave her the power of changing her body twice, and said she would thus see the world and gain experience. Once she changed her body with an old miser for a week; but that she found a great mistake, because, having no soul (only the spirit of a mouse, you know), she felt in an agony of fright all the time. The miser's body was full of nerves, too. He lived in a garret, counting his gold, and was always in fear of robbers. Then his body was full of rheumatism, so she could not hop about as she wished. He had no food she liked. Finally, there was the great enemy in an adjoining room, so that she was a prisoner for a week. However, it was no use her father and I talking to her; she is very wilful, and must suffer and learn by her own experience. I suppose you are young?" she asked.

"Yes," said Jane, "I'm only just in my teens, and very small for my age—I mean in my human body—for I work so hard I fancy my body hasn't time to grow."

"Then my daughter won't find herself in a bed of roses?"

"Oh, dear, no! my bed is stuffed with straw, but there's two blankets, and some poor little girls haven't that. But she'll have to work pretty hard, though it is Sunday."

"I'm glad she won't be too happy, for then, perhaps, she will settle down better with us after this change."

"Are mice republicans, that you say you are the president's wife?" asked Jane.

"Of course we are," it answered, looking very much surprised at Jane's ignorance.

"Is it a parliament sitting there? What are they talking about?"

"Oh, the usual subject! The best way of resisting the great enemy, or, rather, I should say, of eluding him; for unless we are more united, resistance is vain."

Jane looked very serious.

G

"Who—who do you mean by the 'great enemy?'"

"The cat, of course."

"Oh, yes, I had forgotten we were mice," she answered, smiling.

At this minute a cat mewed on the roof; he could not possibly get at the mice, but they all scampered off into different holes. The president's wife pushed Jane into one, followed herself, and told her to "take the first turn to the right, and then straight down."

Jane, however, missed the way, and after many weary hours found herself alone in a dark, damp stone passage. "I think I must be underground now, for it feels like a cellar." There was a tiny crack in a door, through which she saw a light flickering, and she heard men's voices. "I am only a mouse, they won't observe me," she thought, and crept through the crack on to three or four steps, which she had some difficulty in mounting. On the top one she found herself in a strange room she had

never seen before. " I must have come
into another house," she thought, and cau-
tiously skirted the room until she could hide
under a cupboard.   From here she peeped
out to see what the men were doing, as she
wished to find out what kind of place this was.

Three men were sitting round a table
looking at a drawing on it.   One was talking in a low voice, and sitting so that she
could see his face quite plain, for the lamp
on the table shone on his face.   He seemed
to have a horrid, wicked expression ; his hair
was cropped very short, and he had a dirty
white scarf, twisted several times round his
throat.   He was saying to the other two,
whose backs were turned towards her :

"Why not to-night?   When a thing of
this sort has to be done, don't let's put it
off any longer."

"But Rolf says that the old girls sleep.
so light it is impossible to move without
waking them.   It would be far better to do
it on Tuesday when they go to the meeting
for two hours.   Isn't that so, Rolf?"

But before the man thus addressed could answer, the first speaker again interrupted:

"I tell you, I'll have nothing to do with it, unless you'll do it to-night. I've got to go off by the five o'clock train on Monday morning for another job, much bigger than this trumpery half-dozen spoons in an old girl's work-box!"

"Indeed!" said the one they called Rolf; "indeed I do promise you a great, fine prize!"

Jane instantly recognised Mr. Fiddle-whisky's voice to her great surprise. She listened with all her might as he went on.

"I tell you dere is von case containing all the most beautiful zilver plate, belonging to de ladies' brôther. I know, because von of my vriends told me dat they vill not zell it, but keep it vary zafe till dat brôther's return from India. Oh, dey very honour-able ladies! Only vat I zay is, Tuesday is better; Mrs. Hardstick out, too; noting but ——heneral at home—a mere child, a no—t all; and ve can do it in daylight, and leave de case as if untouched Vy! they will not vind out it's gone till de brôther's return. Ha! ha!"

The other man, whose face she could not see, now said:

"If Jim won't join us, except we do it to-night, I vote we settle it to-night, for without Jim we shall only make a mess of it. Look here, Rolf, you've drawn this plan clear enough," and he pointed to the drawing on the table. "Here's the kitchen window. Rolf he opens it from the inside; Jim and I jump in from the back-yard. I stay and watch to give the alarm, if I've reason to think it necessary. I can employ my time cutting out a pane of glass, and wrenching or bending the bar of the shutter, not to let suspicion rest on Rolf for having let us in. Rolf and you, Jim, go in and do the rest."

Mr. Fiddlewhisky here helped himself to a glass of spirits from a bottle on the table, and said:

"Vell, I'll agree, den, for to-night, but,

Jim, you must promise me not to hurt de ladies. I no wish to hang for murder. Ah, no!"

"No fear of that. I'll manage the old girls by threats, while you get out the 'prize,' as you call it. You better not let them see who you are, Rolf. Keep your head in the cupboard."

"Oh, I vill vêre a disguise; my own mothêr would not know me. Besides Mrs. Hardstick and all tink I'm in bed to-day— vâry pad headache. Ah, yes, vâry pad! I must return now secretly. My wife will let me in, when she can do so unobserved, at ten o'clock. It's near that now."

"Well," said Jim, "then, there's an end of this matter. A quarter to two we're in the back-yard, and you, Rolf, unbarring the window. Biggest share for Jim this time, and yours and mine alike. Eh, Rolf?"

"No, no, Jim," he answered; "Jim môst share and share alike. His risk is nothing, but I have great danger. Vy, it vos all my cleverness that planned this! *I* ought to have the biggest share."

They all laughed and got up. Jim said :

"That's what you always say; but you shall only share, and share alike, with us."

"Is that bundle of jewels in there all right?" said the other man, pointing to the door through which Jane had crept in.

"Ay, ay; I've just been counting them. Splendid easy job that was, to be sure!" said Jim.

Jane felt a shiver of horror shake her whole body to the tip of her tail.

"It's the gentlewomen they're going to rob," she said to herself. "Oh, I wish I was myself again. I must, I must run and warn them."

The men took up the lamp and walked through another door. She followed unobserved into a shop where two men were laughing and talking, whilst they turned over a bundle of old boots and shoes on the counter. She did not stop to watch or hear more; she knew enough. Her only wish

was to save the gentlewomen, the dear kind
ladies; but where was she? and how was
she to find her way home? She ran through
the shop into the street. The gas was lit;
it felt cold. She looked up at the sky, but
it was foggy. There were no stars. It
must be near ten o'clock, she thought. She
hesitated a minute, and then ran along the
pavement under the area railings of the
houses until she came to the corner of the
street, and recognised a baker's shop.

"Our baker!" she exclaimed. "Of course
now I know where I am!"

The shop windows were shut, but the
door was half open, and there was a large
sack of flour there, and on it sat—oh,
horror!—a large tortoise-shell cat, licking its
paws.

"Oh," thought Jane, "now here on the
pavement I can't escape; and, if I'm killed,
the gentlewomen won't be saved. Oh dear!
oh dear! what shall I do? If I move, he
may see me."

She turned about her head to look for

some means of escape. There was a little wooden box between the sack and the wall. Without thinking more, she ran in.

" This is safe, it's so small," she thought. " The cat can't get his paw in even, if he did see me."

She turned round with difficulty, it was so small a box. In doing so, she touched something. Snap it went, and she was caught in a trap. The tip of her tail was hurting her very much, for she had not pulled it within the trap.

Here was a misfortune! Now she would probably be drowned like any common, everyday mouse ; and the poor gentlewomen! (even now her kind little heart thought of them), though the men said they would not hurt them, the fright might kill them. Oh, that she might make herself as small as a fly, so that she could crawl out through the bars.

" How stupid not to notice this was a trap! I ought to know one by this time."

So she lamented and blamed herself. The

cat now prowled round the trap, and pawed
it till it turned over. That was very uncomfortable; and she said as loud as she could:

"My tail is caught. Oh, it hurts!"

The baker was deaf, and thought the voice
came from some small boys playing outside
his door; but he soon noticed the cat sniffing
the trap.

"Hullo! caught a mouse again; that's the
tenth to-day. I declare this new trap is the
best kind I've ever had." He picked it up,
and examined the mouse. "What a pretty
mouse! Not a common one at all! Why,
it has large blue eyes, and stares at one
like a Christian. Pity I've no child here to
make a pet of it! I can't kill it; it really
is a pretty mouse!"

Jane's heart beat very hard. She would
not speak for fear of being sold as a
wonder, and kept in a cage all her
life. No, she remembered it would not
be all her life, for at one o'clock she'd
be a girl. Perhaps she had better explain
to the baker. Before she had quite made

up her mind what was the best to do, Mrs.
Hardstick entered.

"I knew," she said, "though your shop
is not open to-day, you'd oblige me with
a cake and a loaf. The mice have eaten
all I bought on Saturday. We are fairly
overrun with the nasty things to-day. I
can't think where they come from."

"Here you are, Mrs. Hardstick," he
answered, and handed down what she
wanted. "Why didn't you send your little
maid? It's late for you to come out such
a night as this, and liable to bronchitis, too,
as you be!"

"Oh, I've had a deal of worry to-day,
Mr. Isaacs; you've no idea! The children
that fretful, and my lodgers that exacting,
I've been fairly run off my legs with one
thing and another. The girl, she's in a
queer way, I can't make her out at all.
Ever since last night she's been took queer-
like, talking and muttering to herself in an
outlandish way, and running downstairs on
all fours, for all the world like a bear!

Yes, indeed, she did once, I watched her! Then she's been asleep all the afternoon in the kitchen screen; curled up like an animal, and me that wild a-looking for her high and low, and wondering if she'd run away! The decayed gentlewomen have been accusing me of cruelty, and say she's only been scared out of her wits by a slap I gave her yesterday, for causing my best lodger to fall. A slap, indeed! It was no more than I've had many times when I was a girl. I say it's the gentlewomen have been spoiling of her. Would you believe it, Mr. Isaacs, when I left home ten minutes ago, the ladies had got her lying down on their own bed, like a queen, with two cushions under her head, and their best India shawl laid over her feet, a-feeding of her with a spoon, and giving her hot chocolate! I shall part with her soon; I can't stand it much longer."

"Oh, well, Mrs. Hardstick, the girl must be ill, for she's always been a quiet, decent girl, when she's come here to get your orders. I'd try what a day of complete rest would do. Here!" he added, as Mrs. Hardstick sighed, and prepared to leave the shop by taking up her umbrella and the parcels, " here, I've caught such a pretty mouse just this minute, and I think your children might like to look at it, it might amuse and keep them quiet for a time. You can return it to me when they are tired of it. I don't want to kill it, see!" he said, holding it up with the light shining on it, "see, it has such peculiar eyes!"

"Yes, so it has!" Mrs. Hardstick said. " Well, thanks, I don't like pets for children, but I'm sure they will like looking at it for a time—it's very kind of you. Talking of eyes,"—and she laid down her parcel in her eagerness to talk to the baker—"talking of eyes—that's the queerest thing of all!—my general servant had pale blue eyes, you know."

"Well," he smiled, " I can't remember; but as she's red hair, I suppose her eyes may be pale."

"Will you believe it? Now they are jet black! Did you ever hear of a box on the ear turning anybody's eyes a different colour? The gentlewomen declare it's because her 'feelings were hurt,' and she's got into some queer 'nervous fever!' Well, what I says is this—it's all queer, I own, but I don't see why *I'm* blamed for all of this."

The baker was getting anxious she should go, so he smiled and handed her the parcels again.

"Give her a day's rest, and promise her she shall have a nice cake for herself, next Sunday, if she's good. I'll give it you free of charge, as you're such an old customer."

"Well, well, good-night!" she said. "You're very kind, I'm sure. I'll take this mouse at any rate for the children to play with to-morrow morning; they are in bed now, for it's awfully late. I was afraid you'd not be in the shop; why, it's past supper time!"

At last she hurried away. Jane was very happy now; she thought that when one o'clock came, she'd be free, and in plenty of time to warn the gentlewomen. She would not speak, for it would startle Mrs. Hardstick too much; she might drop the trap, and run away! The great thing now was to be at home before one o'clock.

When Mrs. Hardstick entered, Miss Angelica came out of her room, saying:

" Jane is snoring! sound asleep again after the chocolate. We are so rejoiced; but we think it right to send for the doctor. My sister has gone to fetch him herself. We intend paying for his visit."

Mrs. Hardstick was not pleased; but she was afraid, after what the ladies had said, that they would think she was unfeeling to Jane. So she said:

" I'm glad the child seems quieter now. May I look?"

" Oh, certainly!"

Mrs. Hardstick put down the trap and umbrella on the table near the bed.

"Well, she does seem peaceful now; but then you've both been that kind, and fussed her up, I'm sure, all this afternoon! I've got some bread and cake you wished for. I fear you've had no supper?"

She put down the loaf and cake on two plates in the cupboard. Then, snatching up the umbrella, and forgetting the trap, she went upstairs, taking a scuttle full of coals with her to the Fiddlewhiskys on the way. Mrs. Fiddlewhisky received it at the door.

"Ah! my dear professor is so bad to-night, he can't bear me even to poke the fire. I vill lay on the coals with my hands. Thank you kindly, Mrs. Hardstick. Good-night."

"Is he not asleep yet?"

"Yes, dozing," and Mrs. Hardstick heard the professor cough. "Hush! that is vy I don't poke," and she closed the door after her very carefully, and locked it.

Mrs. Hardstick went up to the children, and down again to the kitchen. She put out all the gas, and tidied up all the things before going to bed, which she intended doing the moment the doctor had left. The ladies, however, assured her they would let the doctor in, and begged her to go to bed at once.

It was a quarter to one before Dr. Puzzlehead arrived. He was an old man with white hair and a kind face. Miss Angelica showed him straight into their room. He and the gentlewomen began a long whispered conversation near the window. Jane in the trap was still on the table, where Mrs. Hardstick had forgotten her. She could talk in whispers now to the general, and was reproaching her for shamming illness, and giving the gentlewomen so much trouble about nothing.

" Oh, hold your jaw! I've had awful fun all day, particularly since the gentlewomen have petted me, and given me goodies to eat! I say, will you swap with me for good, and remain the mouse ? "

" Certainly not! I must be Jane again. I've got important news to give the gentlewomen."

"Ha! ha!" said the general; "so you're tired of being a mouse already? Well, to tell you the truth, I wouldn't be *you* any longer, for all the cakes in the world! It was all very amusing acting as if I was ill and asleep, but to-morrow I'd have to be well and work. I say, Jane, is that old duffer going to give me physic, do you suppose?"

"I should think it very likely; but you'll be a mouse in ten minutes. I hardly think there'll be time. Oh! by the by, I am very sorry, I've got the tail a little pinched in the trap. It's the only accident I've had," said Jane.

"Well, I must confess I've cut one of the fingers a little bit; but it's sewn up! I hope it won't matter much? My tail will heal in a day, I'm sure."

"Hush!" said Jane, for the doctor came towards the bed.

"Just so—exactly!" he was saying.

The gentlewomen both left the room, one to fetch a hot-water bottle, and the other a tumbler. The doctor took hold of the general's wrist.

" Thirsty, my little girl? "

" No, thank you."

" Just so—feverish ? "

The general began to shake with suppressed laughter, but made no sound.

"Ah ! just so! trembling ? Let me feel your pulse," he said, as he looked at his watch to count. There was a great stillness for a minute, then the clock on the chimney-piece struck *one !*

There was a flutter in the bed. The doctor turned to look, and, oh, wonder! he was holding the paw of a little mouse! He was so surprised he let go, and off the mouse ran ! He was so busy patting and feeling the bed, to see what had become of the girl, that he did not turn or notice the loud sound of something that cracked on the table. The trap was burst, and Jane jumped off the table, and ran out of the door.

" Miss Angelica ! Miss Angelica ! " she called, in a whisper. " I'm quite well, but listen, listen !" she added, panting ; "listen to what I know is going to happen to you !"

The ladies returned, each of them holding one of her hands.

"How's this ? You look quite yourself, my child! We are glad. What have you done, doctor ?"

"I don't quite understand ; but she's well. So I am not wanted any more," and he walked out of the house muttering, "Am I drunk? What is it all? A mouse? No; there was no mouse. There is a girl, and she's perfectly well! I can't make it out! There are some things no doctor can understand!" and he left the house shaking his head.

In the meantime Jane told the ladies all she'd heard. They sat on the sofa, one on each side of her, and did not interrupt her. She told them the mouse had been the general, and she had been in the mouse's body for twenty-four hours ; that she had thus discovered the plot to rob them. These old ladies had such very large hearts that they understood about fairies at once, when Jane explained. They looked into her large blue eyes, and saw she was speaking the truth.

There was no time to be lost. They told Jane at once to fetch the nearest police-man, whilst Miss Amelia took off her shoes, so as not to attract the Fiddlewhiskys' notice, and prepared to go up and warn Mrs. Hard-stick. Miss Angelica blew out her candle, and stood at the front door, hidden behind the cloak and umbrella stand, waiting to let Jane and the policeman in. Both the gentle-women looked very pale, but they were the daughters of a soldier, and the sisters of a soldier, and though they trembled a little because they were old, yet they were as brave as brave.

Jane felt brave also when, at twenty minutes past one, she returned with a police-man. She had found one in a very few minutes. He had whistled for another one, to whom he explained all, and told him to fetch two more. They were to stand in

the back-yard, and watch the two robbers
who were coming there. Miss Amelia had
not been able to warn Mrs. Hardstick; she
said she had not dared to pass the Fiddlewhiskys' door, for she saw a light under it,
and feared they might suddenly come out
and see her. This would have prevented
all their plans for catching the robbers from
being successful. The first policeman hid
himself under the stairs. Jane hid herself
behind the window-curtains of the gentlewomen's room. The ladies both popped
into bed with their clothes on, and pretended to be fast asleep.

Jane wondered how quickly they seemed
to carry out the plan. She stood behind
the window-curtains, and peeped through a
little hole, for they were very old and darned
in many places. The fire was still burning
enough for her to see if anyone came in.
Her heart went pit-a-pat, pit-a-pat, so loud,
she wondered if she'd be able to hear anything else.

Presently the clock struck the half-hour,

and she waited anxiously for ten minutes
more, which seemed an age. She could see
the edge of Miss Amelia's cap—it did not
look a bit like a night-cap—however, a robber
would never notice that, she thought. She
saw little bits of the mouse-trap lying all
over the floor, and on the table. What a
long time it seemed now since she was a
mouse. Could it be really all true that she'd
been a mouse?

Suddenly she heard something at the door.

"Yes," she thought, "it was all true
enough."—She could hear some one standing
listening at the door, probably looking
through the key-hole, so she never moved.
—"Probably it's Mr. Fiddlewhisky listening
to the ladies breathing, but I don't think he
can hear them. I hope he can't hear my
heart. I wish it would be quiet."

Presently the steps came again, and this
time the door opened very gently—for the
ladies never locked their door—and a man
with white hair and beard came in, and
looked towards the bed. Then he turned

and nodded to another man, whom Jane recognised as the robber Jim. They had hardly
entered the room before two policemen appeared, and Jane heard loud talking and
scuffling going on in the kitchen. She jumped
out of the curtain ; the policemen caught hold
of the two robbers. They were so surprised
they did not struggle very much. Jane
pointed to the white-haired man, and said:

" That's Mr. Fiddlewhisky, the other is
Jim."

Mr. Fiddlewhisky's wig had tumbled off,
and there was no use in denying it. Several
policemen came now, so they caught all three
and carried them off to prison, and Mrs.
Fiddlewhisky too.

The ladies felt a little faint after all this
fuss, and Jane attended to them, and said
she'd sleep on the sofa so as to be near if
they wanted something.

Mrs. Hardstick only woke when the robbers
were caught, and then she came to see and
hear everything. She was very much surprised to see Jane quite well, and tucking

up the ladies in bed, and doing everything so nicely. She saw the trap all broken.

"Dear, dear, and Mr. Isaac's mouse escaped, too! Well, it's a mercy we are not all murdered in our beds, I'm sure. I'll never have no foreign folk in my house again."

The ladies did not take the trouble to explain anything about the mouse, or Jane. They knew as Mrs. Hardstick was heartless she would never understand about Jane having saved them and their brother's silver.

Next morning the ladies felt much better; they took hold of Jane's hand and led her to the cupboard, and showed her all the beautiful silver things belonging to their brother. They thanked her, and said they were too poor to give her money, but when their brother returned he would reward her. She kissed Miss Angelica's hand, and said she had felt so very happy to have saved all their things, and to have been useful to them, that she did not want any reward.

Some time after this there drove up a

very grand carriage to the door, and a very,
very old gentleman stepped out, and said
he was the gentlewomen's uncle. He told
them he'd read all about the robbers in the
papers, and was very sorry to find his nieces
were in such poverty. He told them he'd
been very selfish in not inquiring about them
before, and begged them to come and stay
in his house until their brother returned.
After some consultation they agreed to do
so, if they might bring Jane as their little
maid. The old uncle agreed, and next day
he sent his carriage and servants to bring
the gentlewomen and Jane, and the box of
silver, and all their things—including the
cracked cup—to his house.

Jane was a good little maid, and very
clever; the ladies soon said she was a treasure.
She lived happily with them in the old gentleman's house till their brother returned. Then
they all lived in a smaller house, but were
just as happy. Many years after, when the
old ladies died, and she was quite grown up,
they left her enough money to start a lodging-

house of her own. This she did, and had two strong, servant maids, aged twenty, to do all the work. She was very particular who her lodgers were, and very particular that her maids did the work well, but also that they were never overtired.

Of course no one knew of her former life, but the maids thought their mistress rather odd on one matter : which was, that when a mouse was caught in a trap, she always ordered them to bring it to her. She would then carefully examine the tip of its tail, and say :

"It's all right; it's only a common, every-day mouse ; you may drown it, only see it dies quickly or else it's cruel."

And this is the end of the story!

III.

"Lady Fluffy."

NOT very long ago there lived a little girl called Lady Florencia Frederica Theodocia Fancydale. When she was a baby and was beginning to speak, she gave herself the name of "Fluffy," so she was called "Lady Fluffy" all her life. It suited her very well, because her hair was curly and never would lie smooth, and her frock and pinafore being of soft material, edged with frills of lace, would not lie smooth either. She was hardly ever still for one moment during the day, so that she had the appearance of being altogether made of soft, fluffy, fluttering feathers.

She was the youngest of a very large family, but she was not the least spoilt, for all her four sisters and five brothers took care of that—as well as her nurse and governesses, who were very strict.

She learnt many things besides reading, writing, and arithmetic. She was taught music, and drawing, and dancing, and riding, and flying! At least she called it flying. It was really swinging from one stick, hung by ropes to the ceiling, to another, and again on to another. When she did this she looked more like her name than ever. She was not very fond of any lessons that required sitting still for more than five minutes, but, being very inquisitive, she asked many questions, and for her age she really knew a great deal.

Her parents were rich, and lived in a large house. There were many servants and nurses besides the two governesses to look after the children, therefore it is difficult to understand how Fluffy could have the following adventure. However, this is what happened one very hot day in St. James's Park.

She had been playing hide and seek

there with her brothers and sisters. She felt rather tired when it came to her turn to hide, so, running round a clump of shrubs, she sat down on a bench to wait till she heard the others coming to look for her. There was a little girl sitting there also. She paid no attention to her, but listened intently for the sound of her brothers' and sisters' voices. They, however, seemed a long, long time coming. She felt very much bored, so at last, she gave a great jump, screaming out, " Bo ! " to show them where she was.

She had given an enormous jump, it is true, still she was surprised to find she had somehow jumped into a path that seemed strange to her. It was paved with beautiful white pebbles, and on each side there was a high hedge of forget-me-nots, so high, she could not see over it, nor could she understand how she got there.

She walked on a little way, till she came to a large pond full of beautiful fish. In the middle of this water she saw an island with trees, round the edge of which there grew pink and white water-lilies. She was so pleased to see this, and to find herself in so beautiful a garden, that she did not feel frightened at being alone. She only began to consider where she was; she said to herself, "I was in St. James's Gardens, and I thought I knew all the paths; I wonder where I am?"

Presently she heard a step on the gravel behind her, and turning round, she saw a little girl just about her own age, in a cotton frock and pinafore that was patched.

"Are you the gardener's child?" she asked.

"No, I am only a workhouse child; my name is Molly. I have lost my way."

"Oh, have you? How odd, so have I. I can't think where we are. I came through the Green Park from Piccadilly, where we live."

"I came from Birdcage Walk," said Molly, "and meant to go round the water in St. James's Park, but I know all the

paths there, and this is not it. But it is
very pretty, far prettier than anything I've
ever seen."

"Yes, that is just what I was thinking!
I've seen many gardens, but none so beautiful as this. I suppose you are poor? I
mean very poor, as you say you live in the
workhouse?"

"Yes," said Molly, "I am poor; I've got
nothing of my very own."

"I'm so sorry," said Lady Fluffy, as she
took hold of the other little girl's hand.
"I'm very sorry, because it must be dull for
you. I daresay you have never seen pretty
picture books? When I find my way home,
I'll give you some of mine. There are some
fairy stories that you are sure to like, Molly."

"Thank you; that is very kind. What
is your name?" asked Molly, rather shyly;
"you seem quite a lady."

"Oh, yes, of course I am, you know!—at
least, I mean I try to behave like a lady!
My name is Fluffy. But you talk very
nicely, indeed, Molly! And your voice is

pretty and gentle.   Shall we play together?
Or walk about together, just for a time,
until we find our way?"

"Yes, do let us walk together, it will be
fun for a time, though I am sure to be
scolded if I am late going back to the
workhouse; but it is not my fault."

"Oh, no! It's not your fault, I shall
protect you.   Mamma will send somebody
with you to explain to the people at the
workhouse that it only happened because you
were lost! Now, we had better walk back
the way we came, because there is water
here, you see, so we cannot go on."

They went back along the path, which
wound about a good deal between the high
hedges of forget-me-nots, till they soon came
to high iron gates.

"How funny," said Lady Fluffy, "I never
saw those gates when I came along here
before.   I must have jumped very high,
indeed, to have got into this strange place.
Of course, I've had flying lessons, I suppose
that's why I went too far."

ɪ

"Flying   lessons!"   exclaimed   Molly.
"How very nice!   Can you teach me?"

"Yes, I will, by and by; but now, what
shall we do?   Wait at these gates, or go
back by the pond?"

"Let us call first here, perhaps there's
a policeman who will tell us the way."

Scarcely had she said this before they
saw one on the other side of the bars, but
he was quite small, not much taller than
they were, although with a quite grown-up
appearance.

"Which is the best way to Piccadilly,
please?" asked Fluffy.

"I know of no such place here; you
can't come through these gates, they are
locked; but if you want to go towards your
ideal, walk straight back the way you came."

"But there's a pond, and we saw no boat;
how can we cross?"

He took a gold whistle out of his pocket,
and blew it.

"All right, ladies, you'll find the boat there
now."

They thanked him, and turned.

"What an unusual man!" whispered Fluffy. " Fancy a policeman not knowing where Piccadilly is! And what did he mean by our 'ideal'? I am puzzled, Molly, but it is no good wondering over things one don't quite understand. He was not an every-day policeman, for he was so small, and he had a gold whistle. I am puzzled," she repeated, as she walked hurriedly on.

The moment they came to the edge of the pond again, they saw a boat appear from under the overhanging trees on the island, coming straight across towards them. It came of itself, and had no oars. It was painted green, and had soft silk cushions on the seat.

Lady Fluffy took Molly's hand, and they both stepped into it. When they were seated, it took them straight to the other shore, and landed them on dry sand just above the water-lilies. As they walked up on the bank, they saw two ponies, ready saddled, tied to a tree.

"This is delightful, Molly! Now, we can have a ride."

"Are you sure they are meant for us?"

"I think so; besides, my motto is 'Nothing venture, nothing have.' Which will you ride? The brown or the white?"

"I think," said Molly, "the brown looks the quietest, and I've never ridden before, so if you don't mind I would rather try that."

Lady Fluffy helped Molly on to it, and jumped up on to the white pony herself. The path was rough and stony that led up into what they supposed was the island, so they could only go slowly. They had not gone far before they found themselves in a large wood, and began to think it could not be an island.

"It must be a promontory, I think," said Fluffy. "Have you, Molly, ever felt you would like to do something grand?" she went on; "I mean, fight battles? or save some princess that an ogre had tied to a tree? or something of that sort?"

"No, I have never thought about those

things ; but I should like—at least, up till now
I've thought I should like—to be a cook !
A grand cook, you know ! who makes dinners
for great people, and then I should have
several maids to obey me."

" How very funny you are, Molly ! A
cook ? Why, then you could not travel about
or see new countries. Don't you like riding,
now ? "

" Oh, yes, I like riding with you, Fluffy ;
indeed, I would follow you anywhere ; only, it
is all so new and strange."

When they had ridden some time up
through the wood, they came to a wide heath,
and Fluffy held Molly's pony for fear she
should be frightened, as now the ponies
galloped over the common till they came to
a very high wall.

" This must be a small town, and here are
the walls," said Fluffy ; "only, where are the
gates ? We shall have to ride round till we
find them."

So they did, till they saw an arch in the
wall, and wooden gates that were closed.

Over them under the arch was written in large letters, " Nothing venture, nothing have."

" My motto," said Fluffy, and without getting off her pony she pulled the bell.

A child like themselves peeped out of a window they had not observed before, and asked them what they wanted.

" We have lost our way ; we should like to come in and have tea, and perhaps someone will show us the way home ? "

The child did not answer, but they heard her call to someone, and instantly the gates were opened by two little boys all in armour, with helmets on their heads, and swords hanging to their sides. Fluffy rode in and bowed her thanks, followed by Molly, who had to kick her pony gently to make it go on, for it was rather tired.

Now they found themselves in an old-fashioned town, the streets were narrow and the houses high. All the inhabitants were children ; none of them were less than five or more than twelve. The market-place was full of different coloured booths, where buying and selling was going on. No one seemed to notice them as they rode through this place, until they came to the steps of the principal house. Here two little girls, with crowns made of roses on their heads, were standing, and they clapped their hands with joy, and said:

"At last you have come, Lady Fluffy!" and pointing to Molly, they said: "And Molly, too, is welcome, the little workhouse girl! Oh, we have been expecting you both for a hundred years!"

"I don't understand," said Fluffy; "and do tell us, how do you know who we are?"

"You will understand all by and by; but now come in and have tea with us," and the two grooms took their ponies, and jumping off, they followed the two little rose-crowned girls into their palace.

It was beautiful! The hall which they entered first was hung round with pictures of all the brave things that children had done. There was the Spartan child that carried the fox, whilst it nibbled and bit him; and Jack the giant-killer; and William Tell's son with the apple on his head, smiling, confident that his father's arrow would hit the apple, and that he would remain unhurt. There were many more pictures of this kind; but Fluffy had not time to admire them all. She explained one or two to Molly, as they walked slowly through the hall to a smaller room.

Here tea was spread out on a table for four, with chairs arranged all ready. Fluffy and Molly were very hungry, so they ate and drank, while their two hostesses talked about the pictures in the hall, which was very interesting to Fluffy and quite new to Molly.

After tea, Fluffy asked if the rose-crowned ones would tell them their names.

" We are twins, and our names are White-rose and Pink-rose, but we have an elder sister called Red-rose. She is in prison, and you, Lady Fluffy and Molly, are the only beings who can restore her to us."

Fluffy was delighted, for she said :

" I have always wished for adventures, and I shall be glad to do my best to save your sister. Who is the cruel person who has imprisoned her?"

"That is what we have never known. Our country is small, you see—it consists only of this town and a very little piece of land outside. A hundred years ago we were all three making an expedition into a friend's country not far from here. But just as we left our frontier, a cloud of dust appeared in front of us, and approached so rapidly, that we had only time to throw our veils over our heads, and wait until the cloud should have passed us. Red-rose was on our right, and she said: 'I hear chariot wheels! Who can it be?' Then we heard a whip crack, and a carriage and horses gallop past; but the dust blinded us, we saw nothing. When we opened our eyes again, Red-rose had vanished! We are sure she was carried away. You must understand," she continued, "that all of us being children, we have to be very careful when we leave our town. For lonely people, who have no children of their own, often come roaming round about our country to see if they can catch some of our subjects, and carry them to their lonely homes, to amuse and cheer them. Red-rose must have been carried away by someone of this kind, and finding she was a princess, perhaps they wanted to make her give up several of her subjects in her stead. Had she promised to do this, no doubt they would have let her return; but, of course, our sister is too good and noble to do such a thing, even to save herself."

White-rose looked very sad when she told them this story.

Fluffy asked: "Have you no idea in what direction she is?"

"Yes, once she was able to send us a few lines written on a leaf, which was screwed up and stuck into an apple. A kind fairy dropped it in our garden as she passed. Our sister told us therein that you and Molly would come here when a hundred years were passed, and that we were to tell you to go towards the west, to a castle where she is imprisoned in a secret turret."

After giving them many instructions, White-

rose took Fluffy into another room, where a
suit of armour was ready for her. She put
it on, and also a helmet on her head. Then
White-rose gave her a sword, on the handle of
which was engraved Fluffy's favourite motto.
This suit of armour was all so neat and small
she felt quite comfortable in it, and when she
looked into the glass she exclaimed ;

"See! ¡Don't I look like Joan of Arc,
only not near so big?"

" No, you are only a child like all of us ; but
if you are brave and do all we've told you, you
will surely overcome the difficulties."

In the meantime Molly had been taken by
Pink-rose to another little room, and had put
on different clothes also ; but she was not so
changed in appearance, as she looked just like
a little cook, with a neat cap and apron.
Pink-rose had thrown over her a dark blue
cloak lined with red, and it had a hood; it
made her look grown-up. Also she had given
her a very long spoon, which would be very
useful to her, she said. They were not told
exactly what dangers they would have to en-

counter; they only knew they would have much to do before the princess could be saved.

As the sun was setting, the princesses ordered the ponies round to the front door again. Fluffy and Molly mounted them, and, waving their hands, bade them adieu, and rode slowly out of town by the same gates through which they had entered.

" Now," said Fluffy, " we must gallop again ; but I need not hold your reins, because you seem quite accustomed to riding now, Molly."

" Yes, I feel quite comfortable, my pony is so gentle and good. You're right; we must go fast, so as to do what we can before the night comes on."

Fluffy spurred her pony, and away they went like the wind towards the west, where in the distance the golden sun was fast sinking into huge dark clouds, all edged with red. The light was still so bright they could hardly see where they were going. The path that led across the common was wet with a recent shower, and reflected the light so strongly that it seemed to them like a golden winding river, ending in the sky.

"It's no use trying to see where we're going to at present," said Fluffy, shading her eyes with her hand; "we must trust to our ponies."

"Presently the sun will go down," said Molly, "and then we shall see if we are near our journey's end." But scarcely had she said it before she added, "What is that glittering in the distance? It looks like a troop of horse-guards coming towards us. What shall we do? We are only two, and they seem many."

Fluffy and Molly reined in their steeds to watch what seemed to them a moving mass of glittering lances coming along the winding road.

"No, it's not soldiers," said Fluffy. "It seems all one thing, whatever it is. For see now it turns with the road; there's its tail. Now, Molly, we must be brave. It's a serpent, or a dragon, or something very terrible."

"Oh, how horrible!" said Molly. "I see now what I thought were lances or swords flashing in the sunlight are spikes sticking up all along its back. It is a monster. What shall we do?"

"Well, Molly, we must face it. Whatever happens, we must not show we are frightened. Perhaps, if we gallop very fast, we may pass it without its eating us: Once we've passed it we shall be safe, for it's so very long that it will take some time to turn round and follow us. We must start now, Molly. You keep to its left side, and I will pass by on the right side."

"It has a thousand legs," said Molly, who was beginning to tremble; "but I will be brave. Only do let's shout something as we pass; that always helps one."

"Yes, we'll shout," said Fluffy, "and that may frighten it."

So she spurred her pony on to a gallop, and Molly flourished her large spoon in the air, and away they went.

Fluffy unsheathed her sword, ready to thrust

into the monster should it try to devour either
of them. As they approached, they felt a
horrible hot wind that came and went in puffs,
and seemed to suck up all it met. This was
the monster's breath, which felt like a whirl-
wind, as Fluffy galloped past, shouting as loud
as she could :

"St. George for merry England !"

It put out its tongue to catch her, but she
slashed a bit off with her sword as she passed.
She nearly fell off her saddle in doing so, for
the pony shied with fright. When she got
past its tail, she turned to see if Molly was
safe, but to her great grief she was nowhere
to be seen.

Molly had meant to gallop past on the left
side, and was shouting, "St. George for—";
but, before she could say "for merry England," she was in the animal's mouth, pony and
all. She still held the spoon straight up, and
it was such a strong one that it kept the
monster's mouth from closing or hurting her.
The teeth were all round her like jagged rocks
in a cavern; but she sat still on her pony un-

hurt on the middle of its tongue, and the spoon
stuck right up into its palate. Molly was
frightened, being in such danger, and the noise
in the animal's throat was fearful—like the
roaring of many wolves. He struggled to spit
Molly out, for she and her pony were far too
big a mouthful, but in vain. There she was
stuck.

In the meantime Fluffy turned back the
moment she missed her companion, and soon
understood what had happened, by the animal's
mouth being wide open, and by the coughing
and choking noise he was making. He seemed
paralysed. All his claws were no help to him,
and he lay flat on his stomach, his legs spread
out on each side, puffing and panting.

"Now is my opportunity," said Fluffy to
herself, and she got off her pony, who instantly
began to graze by the side of the road. She
then climbed on to the monster's back, beginning at the tail, where it was easier, helping
herself along by the spikes that were sticking
out of its back. Once when she did so, as
she approached his neck, she fancied she heard

a voice underneath saying, "Hulloo! Something has got hold of my bayonet"; but she thought it must be a mistake on her part. The monster's breathing whistled and roared so loudly, it was no wonder she heard odd sounds.

When she got on the nape of his neck, she unsheathed her sword and struck him with all her might just behind the right ear. There was a noise like thunder, but she struck again behind the left ear. The animal writhed under her and then died, whilst the head rolled off, with Molly still inside the mouth. Fluffy slid off the animal, and helped her and her pony out from between the teeth. They were a little sprinkled with blood, but there was a stream close by, so they soon made themselves tidy again.

When they stepped back into the road, they were very much surprised to see a troop of twenty soldiers with bayonets, who had cut their way out of the monster's body. They each came and knelt on one knee before Fluffy, and, kissing her hand, they thanked her for having saved them. They had all been swallowed by the monster. Very likely, not being on horseback like Molly, they had slipped through his neck easily. Once in the body, they had all poked up their bayonets through his back; but this did not seem to hurt the animal, and they had been carried on thus, they thought, for days.

Fluffy made them all a little speech, saying she was very happy to find that, in saving Molly, she had also released them, and that, in return, she hoped they would help her to rescue the Princess Red-rose.

At this they gave three cheers for Lady Fluffy, and promised to obey her until the princess was restored to her sisters.

During all this time the two ponies were quietly grazing, and Molly was walking round the monster, examining his flesh to see what it was like, and suddenly she called out :

" I'm sure his paws are good to eat ! We are all very hungry, shall I cook them for you ? "

To this they all agreed, and each soldier cut

off a paw, and brought it to her. She touched each with her spoon, and ordered them to be spitted on bayonets. A fire was lit, and two soldiers turned the weapons round and round over it, until they were nicely browned. She then patted each with her spoon and dished them up on large leaves that grew near at hand. All agreed they were excellent, and tasted something between sheeps' trotters and turtle.

When they had eaten enough, Fluffy said it was time to move on. The sun had gone down and the moon was beginning to shine. There were no trees, and there were no mounds or hills, from the tops of which they might have seen where the road led to. Molly suggested they might put all the pieces of the monster's body together on a heap, climb on the top, and thus see what they could see. This they did, and Fluffy, who had very long sight, said she saw a river in the distance, and, on the other side, a hill.

"I am sure the princess is hidden in a castle or prison on the other side of that rising

ground.   It is very like the country the sisters
described to us," she added, turning to Molly.

They followed the road that led to the river.
The soldiers could not march very fast, so
Fluffy and Molly made their ponies go very
slowly, keeping well on in front.

They knew there were more dangers to en-
counter, but, having overcome such a large
monster, they had more confidence in the
future.   When they came to the river, they
found the bridge was broken down.   Doubtless the monster had done this.   The river
was too deep to wade, and only Fluffy and one
or two of the soldiers had learnt to swim.
Fluffy considered a little time, and then she
ordered the soldiers to lie down on the broom
or heather, and rest for some hours of the
night.   " By dawn I shall tell you what to do,"
she said.   Molly shared the large blue cloak
with her, and they also lay down in the driest
part of the road they could find.

Molly, however, woke up again in the
middle of the night.   The moon was still
shining, and she saw all were fast asleep.

Now, she thought she would like to do some great thing to help on the expedition. So she gently disengaged herself from her cloak, leaving Fluffy wrapped up in it, and taking her spoon, she went softly down to the river's edge, and stared into it.

It was certainly very, very deep. "If there was not such a quantity of water, I'd try to ladle it out with my fairy spoon! but even for that, there is far too much!" Whilst saying this to herself, she dipped the spoon in and let the water run over it. The spoon fell from her hand into the river, but she was not alarmed at this, for it hung by a tape to her belt. She pulled the tape, but felt some resistance. "A fish has caught my spoon," she said, and pulled with all her might, but still she could not get it back.

She became very much frightened now, for she feared that whatever it was that held the spoon, she would not be able to pull it out again, and perhaps it might pull her in. She did not dare leave go, for she knew that without her spoon she would be unable to do anything. It had saved her life already, and had made the monster's paws into good food for them all. She set her feet against a stone, and pulled again with all her strength, and this time, quite suddenly, up came the spoon, and hanging to it was a rope, the noose of which was slung round it. She had pulled with such force, that when it came up with a jerk, she had fallen backwards; however, she soon jumped up and tugged at the rope, which seemed easy work now—then there appeared the keel of a boat!

She was so pleased and excited she called to the others to wake up. Helter-skelter they all came running. Fluffy was the last, and ordered the soldiers to help Molly. A beautiful large boat it was. And as day now began to dawn, all was ready for them to cross the river.

The boat only held five or six, so it had to go backwards and forwards four times before all had crossed. Molly was the boatman, because there were no oars, so she stood up and guided it across with her spoon.

"Really, I think, Molly, you overcome difficulties with your spoon better than I do with my sword!" said Fluffy.

"Shall we exchange?" said Molly, laughing, for she knew Fluffy would not part with her sword for anything.

"No; let's go on as we are. I'm a soldier, and you're a cook," she answered. "But what shall we do with the boat? We shall want it for our return."

Molly suggested to let it go, and see what would happen, which was soon settled, for the instant they let go it slipped under the water and disappeared.

They had left the ponies tied to a rock on the other side, and these seemed quite contented to wait.

Fluffy marched on in front of the soldiers, and shouted out the order to "Shoulder arms," and Molly followed the last, shouldering her spoon. They walked on thus for some time silently, till they came to the hill.

"Now," said Fluffy, "Molly and I will go up in front and reconnoitre,"

She told the soldiers to "Stand at ease," whilst they climbed up.

It was a short but steep ascent. When they got to the top, they saw a castle about two miles off in the plain below them, and all around it lovely orchards. Some of the apple trees were covered with fruit, and some still covered with blossom.

" How pretty!" they both exclaimed.

The castle had two gates, one to the north, and one to the south.

" Listen to me!" said Fluffy. "I see quite plainly what we ought to do. You, Molly, take ten soldiers, and enter the south gate, whilst I and the other ten go round to the north gate. Thus the inhabitants will be more alarmed, for they will imagine two armies have come upon them at once. Let's be quick before they wake up. It is still quite early in the morning."

Molly agreed. They turned back, and ran down the hill to tell the soldiers. They did not like to shout, for fear of rousing someone who might be watching hidden in the orchards.

However, the soldiers were nowhere to be seen.

"Perhaps they have deserted us!" said Molly, quite distressed.

"Never!" said Fluffy. "They are Englishmen, and would never break their word! Perhaps they are lying asleep in the grass. You know I said 'Stand at ease,' and they may have 'Sat down at ease.' It's all the same thing."

In spite of her words, however, she looked very uneasy, as they came nearer to the very spot where they had left the soldiers, and no trace of them could be found.

"I think," said Fluffy, "if I was to shout 'To arms!' it might bring them, if they are hiding or sleeping in the grass. I've given no command yet, you see."

She drew her sword and shouted "To arms!" but there was no movement to be seen, and no sound to be heard, save a little rustling of the breeze among the grass.

"Something has happened to them; but I won't believe they have deserted," she said very sadly, leaning on her sword, whilst a tear or two trickled down her cheek.

Molly put her hand on her shoulder, and said:

" I am so sorry ; but don't cry ! Perhaps, for some reason we can't understand, they have thought it better to go round the hill into the orchard."

" Oh, no," said Fluffy. " Soldiers ought not to *think*, but *obey !* "

"Well, Lady Fluffy, you and I were alone when we met the monster ; and now we are alone again, but no worse off than we were. *I* will never leave you ! "

" True, Molly. You are a faithful friend ; and we two alone will try to rescue the princess."

So saying, she went up the hill again, followed by Molly. When from the top they looked over the orchard, there was no trace of the soldiers.

" They are not here. Let us not part, but go together first to the south gate ; and if we cannot enter there, then we'll try the north," said Molly.

When they got to the middle of the orchard, it became thick with the leaves and twigs. The branches of the apple trees were so impenetrable that it was quite dark, and they could no longer see in which direction to go.

"We must pick off some leaves, and make a peep-hole," said Molly.

"Yes," said Fluffy; "it's tiresome, for it will take some time," and she began to make a hole in front of her face: Presently she called out: "Here are such a quantity of caterpillars helping me, see! How quickly they nibble off the leaves!"

"So there are here," said Molly. "There are about nine or ten helping me. The funny thing is, I noticed them clinging to me for some time past, but I did not like to shake them off, for they are such pretty caterpillars."

They were large, brown and red, hairy caterpillars, and they worked so hard that soon the two girls could see out through the thicket, and perceived that they were not far from the castle.

" Now we had better climb through the holes
we have made in the branches, and try to get
into more open ground," said Fluffy.

With great difficulty they scrambled on until
they reached a meadow, and not far in front
of them stood the castle walls. They were
quite wet with the morning dew, and covered
with blossom off the apple trees. When they
reached the south gate, Molly blew into the
horn that hung there instead of a bell.

" Are you the doctor?" said a voice from
within.

" Are you in want of one?" asked Fluffy,
avoiding an untruth.

" Yes, for my master is ill; but who are
you?"

" Open the door and you will see."

" Certainly not. My orders are to open the
door to no one unless he is a doctor."

Molly whispered to Fluffy to come away
and let her speak instead; so they walked
away, keeping close under the wall till they
reached the north gate.

" Now let me speak," said Molly, "and

hearing another voice they may let us in."

"You shall speak, but you can't pretend to be a doctor, Molly, for you only are a little girl."

"Now, let me manage this, and you will see."

So saying, she blew into the horn. Instantly there came the sound of a patter-patter of footsteps, like someone walking on wet stones in soft slippers.

"What is it?" said the same voice.

"I am Molly, and am travelling with a friend. We have been walking since early dawn. Do let us in, and you will be rewarded."

"Who is Molly? That does not sound like a doctor's name. No, no, go away. I can only admit a doctor, for my master is ill."

"But we are weary; do let us in! I can perhaps cure your master, for I am a cook, and can make dishes that are not only delicious, but that cure many illnesses."

"Ah, that alters the case. Wait, and I will ask the master," and the steps went away;

"But now what will happen if your dish does not cure him?" whispered Fluffy.

"Do not fear! I have perfect trust in my spoon."

They had not many minutes to wait before they heard the pitter-patter-splash again within, and the door was opened by an enormous frog, taller than they were. Fluffy put her hand to her sword, and Molly grasped her spoon, as they both were startled at this unusual sight; but, being very brave, of course, they entered the gate boldly, following the frog. They were shown into a large, dark room, hung round with leopard and lion skins, and on a couch in the corner there lay a large something huddled up in fur.

"That is the king," said the frog to Molly; "but your friend, the knight in armour, had better follow me. I will give him food whilst my master tells you his symptoms."

For a moment Molly hesitated, and Fluffy said:

"Let me stay and help you."

Molly glanced at her spoon, and then winked at Fluffy.

" When Molly had let in a ray of light."   [*Page* 159.

"No; I must be alone with my patient, only come if I call."

She understood that Molly wished to keep her eye on the owner of the castle, whilst Fluffy should, in the meantime, watch outside, and find out how many lived here, and where it was likely the princess might be hidden. So she nodded to her friend and followed the frog.

Groans, in the meantime, came from the bundle in the corner, and Molly approached.

" I fear you are suffering great pain, sir ? "

" Pain ? " said a hollow voice. " I should think so !—agonies ! "

" Where ? " she asked.

" Oh ! just now a biting pain has come on in my big toes and my ears, also in my nose, but this pain is new ; some hours ago I had only an ache in my body."

" It's so dark, sir, I can't see you. May I open the shutter ? "

" Yes," he answered, groaning again.

When Molly had let in a ray of light on to the couch, she saw a large man's head, with an apple in the place of his nose, and two green apple leaves instead of ears, and a stalk sticking up out of the top of his bald head. At first she was so surprised she could only say, "Oh! oh!" and this annoyed him.

"What are you staring at? Have you never seen an orchard king before? Perhaps," he added, "I look less like a king now as I've not got on my crown. You see, I'm too ill to care for my appearance. Now, do be quick, and find out the cause of my pain. Look—look at my ears—they hurt the most just now; or shall I show you my tongue?"

"Oh, no, thank you! I'll examine your ears," and she bent over him.

In a moment she understood what was the matter, for she saw five caterpillars nibbling each leaf, which were his ears. Of course they were her friends come again. She remembered having seen a great many tumbling off Fluffy's and her dress whilst standing at the south gate, and she had noticed they crept under the door. That was doubtless the time they attacked the orchard king. Now she saw that whenever he wiped them away with his horny hands, they kept returning and nibbled again. His skin was so hard he never felt the soft hairy little things crawling about him. She thought the same might be going on at his toes.

"Allow me," she said, and gently lifted the covering at his feet.

She was right, for both big toes were large apples, and caterpillars were crawling over them. Then she glanced at her spoon, and saw written on it the name of the illness she was to call it.

"I see, sir, you are suffering from acute gluttonic-applo-indulgiana symptoms."

"Well, never mind its name," he said; "but cure it."

Now, Molly knew the new pain, as he called it, would be cured if she carried off all the caterpillars; but that was not why she and Fluffy had come. She did not wish to cure him until the princess was saved. So she consulted her spoon again, and called out to the frog to bring six eggs, some cream, sugar, and a pudding-dish. Then she took a piece

L

of string, and persuaded the invalid to let her tie his hands together.

"You keep rubbing your nose and ears with your fingers, and you will make them worse. Now, the string will just keep your hands together, and remind you not to do so."

"Oh! but they tickle! And oh! how they hurt!" he screamed; but he let her tie his hands. Then she pretended to look at his feet again, but really she whispered to the caterpillars:

"Leave off biting his toes, my friends, and tell the others only to torment him if he tries to get up."

They seemed to understand, for presently the orchard king sighed, and said:

"Certainly, I'm better already. Do you know since you've tied my hands, my nose and ears are better, and my toes are quite well, only I still feel the old pain—oh, the old pain in my body! but that, I know, comes from eating apples in this month. They were cursed by a fairy, and, at this time, disagree with me. Yesterday was the last day of

that month, and so I ventured ; but you see
how ill it has made me! Oh, but I do feel
better, though!   I'd like to sit up," and he
put down one foot to the ground, and began
to rise. "Oh! the pain, the pain in my toe!
Oh! now it's in my nose, too! Oh! oh! my
ears! my ears! Oh, dear! oh, dear!" and he
sank back into bed again.

Molly said firmly :

"I must insist on your keeping quiet. It is
very important not to move, for now you will
be soon cured. Soon I will make you a nice
dish," she added, as the frog entered, bringing
the things she'd asked for.

The creature stood looking on whilst she
broke the eggs, sprinkled the sugar, and began
whipping them up with her spoon.

"Would you like to taste what I am making
for your master?"

"Very much," said the frog, "if there's any
left when he has done."

Fluffy stood now at the door; the frog never
noticed her.

Then Molly poured in the cream, and it did

look very tempting whilst she fed the king with her spoon.

At the first mouthful he said, "Good!" at the next he said, "Delicious!" at the third he said, "Exquisite!" at the fourth he said, "I will reward you!" at the fifth he said, "By telling you a secret!" at the sixth he said, "In the left hand drawer of that writing-desk!" at the seventh mouthful he went on, "There is a key which opens a box on the stairs—" at the eighth mouthful, "In it you'll find a tiger's tooth—" at the ninth spoonful his voice was more feeble, and he said, "It's a charm, and opens any door—" at the tenth he seemed half conscious, and was only able to murmur, "Door, if—one taps—" and then he slept.

Fluffy darted forward towards Molly:

"See," she said, "the frog has been eating it while you weren't looking!"

Molly turned to look, and there lay the frog on the floor fast asleep, too. The caterpillars were crawling, and kept tumbling off the couch now. Flop, flop, they came on to the floor.

"Oh, don't let the caterpillars touch the dish

or they will become unconscious also, and they have been so kind and useful."

"Come away, quick," said Fluffy; "let's look for the charm. Do leave the caterpillars to sleep if they like," she added.

But Molly began picking them up, saying:

"It won't take a minute. Really, you don't know how they've helped us."

So Fluffy bent down, too, and gathered them up.

"There's just twenty; but one has eaten a drop that was spilt on the carpet. Look, Molly, it's asleep!"

"Poor little thing! I'll put it in my pocket." And she popped it in the pocket of her apron.

"Do let's be quick, before they wake," said Fluffy. "I've found out a secret tower where I think the princess is, but the door is locked, and I can't see a keyhole."

"Wait," said Molly, "we must find the charm first, and see if we can open it with that."

After finding the key they ran out to the

chest in the passage, and when, with great
difficulty, they opened the heavy lid, they saw
it was half full of pearls, rubies, emeralds, and
sapphires, all mixed up, and lying like gravel
in a heap.   They did not wish to lose time for
fear the orchard king should awaken, but they
admired this treasure, passing their hands all
about to find the charm.

Suddenly Fluffy found a small, round box
with a tiger's head painted on it, and set in a
frame of pearls and rubies.

"We will take nothing from him, not even
this box, which contains the charm, I think.
Is it not pretty, Molly?"

"Yes, it is beautiful; we had better not look
at it long, or we might wish to keep it!"

Fluffy unscrewed the box, and took out the
tooth that lay within on red velvet.

"Here   is   the   charm.   Now   for   the
tower!"

Down   they   rushed   to   the   kitchen,   and
Fluffy remarked:

"It is a good thing there are no servants!
There appeared to be no living being when I

was looking about, whilst the frog got the eggs and things you asked for."

She went straight to the shutter of one of the windows, and disappeared behind it, calling to Molly to follow.

They climbed up a narrow stone stair inside the wall that led them up to a small turret, and here was an iron door without handle or key-hole. Fluffy tapped it with the tiger's tooth three times, but it did not open.

" He said 'tap,' didn't he ? "

"Yes," said Molly; " but he fell asleep before he told us what to tap. Perhaps it's the floor; try that!"

But, no, that was not it. Presently a feeble voice within asked :

" Who knocks? Friend or foe ? "

"We are friends," Fluffy answered, " and we've come to save Princess Red-rose. Is she here ? "

" Yes," the voice answered, " for I am that princess most certainly ! "

" Well, we've got the charm, but we don't know how to use it, and the door is locked ! "

"Alas," said the princess, "I never saw how the orchard king opened it. He came only once a week to bring me bread and water; but I fear you are risking your life in trying to save mine. Don't you know there's a terrible monster who devours people? He is sure to gobble you up! Indeed, I wonder how you ever got here, for he watches all night, and most of the day, and seldom sleeps. How was it you escaped?"

They heard her press close to the door as she asked this, and her voice was not that of a child.

Fluffy whispered to Molly:

"Shall we tell her we've killed him? Can she really be Princess Red-rose? Her voice is not like a child's."

"Yes; tell her you killed him. It's all right; she is the elder sister, and may be grown up."

Then they heard the voice again:

"Ah, I hear you whispering; you will leave me. I don't blame you; only fly away quickly before the monster sees you."

"No, no; we will try and save you. Think no more of the monster; he is dead, cut up into many pieces. We conquered and killed him last night."

"What! You killed him? Then you are Lady Fluffy and your friend is Molly. Hurrah! hurrah! You are indeed come to save me! But where is the orchard king, and his frog?"

Molly answered, "Asleep, both! I made a dish which has sent them off in a deep slumber, but I know not how long it may last. Oh, princess! can't you suggest to us how to use the charm? It's a tiger's tooth, and the king was unconsciously telling us what to do when he fell asleep—his last words were, 'tap'!"

"And," said Fluffy, "we have tapped the door, and tapped the floor three times, it's no good. Oh! what shall we do?"

"Try," the princess said, after a minute's pause, while she thought, "try tapping your own forehead three times with it."

Fluffy did so, and instantly the door rose up

into the ceiling, and they saw a *little old woman* standing before them! She had a kind but wrinkled face, and on her grey hair was a wreath of faded roses, red no more, but dark brown and withered. There was a faint smell of dead rose leaves as she stepped forward, holding out her arms to embrace them; but Fluffy and Molly were so surprised, they could not move.

At last Fluffy said, "Are you really the sister of White-rose and Pink-rose?"

"Yes! Why do you doubt me? why! oh, why do you look so disappointed? Oh, Lady Fluffy, let me press you to my heart, and Molly also, for I love you both so much for coming to save me!"

Fluffy and Molly then came and kissed her.

And one said, "We are glad to have found you, only—"

And the other added, "Only we expected a little child like your sisters, and we are just a little — surprised!" And both little girls blushed, and tears came to their eyes.

The princess was very, very old, and had no

trace of beauty left, whilst the faded wreath gave her a piteous appearance.

"Am I not like my sisters? I am only a year older than they; but, of course, it's a hundred years since I saw them, and my wreath must be faded, though I have never seen myself in a glass. Is it faded?" she asked.

Fluffy and Molly were dreadfully disappointed at finding, after all their struggles, they had only rescued a very old princess, who looked as if she would die soon; but they did not like to hurt her feelings, so they each took her hand and said:

"Your wreath is faded certainly, and you do look older than we expected, but we wish to save you, dear princess! So come now, quickly!"

She managed to get down the secret stairs, and Fluffy ran into the king's room, and placed the box containing the charm in his hand. One hurried glance at him and the frog, showed her that both still slept. Then she returned to help Molly to lead Red-rose

out of the castle.   As they passed through the
passage that led to the north gate, the princess
stopped before a looking-glass and screamed :

"Who is that little ugly old woman ?   Not
me, surely not me ? " and then she burst into
tears.   " Oh, how wretched I am !   I am old !
I am old, and no longer the pretty little Red-
rose—and yet I feel so young—quite a child,
like you and Molly.   Oh, what shall I do?   It
is terrible to feel young, and be withered like
this ! " and she tore off her wreath, and flung
it on the ground.

Fluffy and Molly both kissed her.

" Come away," they said, " come away quick,
before the king wakes.   Your sisters will love
you just the same."

They said this to cheer her, but they thought
all the same how shocked the little sisters
would be when they saw such a very old
woman come back, instead of the pretty princess Red-rose.

They had to support her when she got out
into the meadow, she seemed weak and
faint.

" If I could have something to eat I should feel stronger."

Molly promised to try and make her a nice dish when they had crossed the river again ; but they did not dare to let her eat any apples whilst they climbed through the enchanted orchard, for fear of the effect they might have.

When they had climbed the top of the hill the air revived them all. Even the princess seemed better able to walk without their assistance. Then they descended to the spot where the soldiers had disappeared ; but it all looked just the same, and there was no trace of them.

When within sight of the river, Molly ran on to fish up the boat with her spoon. All went well, the boat came up, and they three went across in it. Before the boat touched the other shore, Fluffy said :

" By the by, I wonder if the caterpillars are all right ? The handkerchief I am carrying them in feels to me to be getting heavier and heavier ! "

" Well," said Molly, " it's very strange, but the sleepy one in my pocket feels just as heavy

as a stone! Do you think they have died?
Poor things, I should be sorry! Perhaps we
should have left them on the hill in the grass,
that is the place they came from."

When they landed and got out, the boat
slipped back into the water as before. Fluffy
now put down the handkerchief containing the
caterpillars on the bank, and began undoing
the knot.

"They certainly feel heavy, more so even
than if they were dead mice. And after all, if
I remember right, I had only nineteen, and
you, Molly, carried the sleepy one."

"Yes," said Molly, and she took off her
apron and laid it on the ground. "Take care
not to hurt them in undoing that knot; let me
do it."

The knot was very difficult to untie, and the
caterpillars inside seemed as large as mice, and
quite as lively, jumping and kicking At last
it was undone, and nineteen little men rolled
out, laughing and struggling.

Fluffy and Molly stared at them, speechless
with astonishment, for they stood up in a row,

and grew and grew until they were full-grown soldiers, with bayonets, just as they were before. This time they knelt down on one knee, and not only kissed Fluffy's hand, but Molly's, too. Then they explained all to the princess, and she thanked the soldiers. She assured them their sleeping companion would soon wake after entering the town where she lived.

As there was now no fear of pursuit, and they all felt exhausted and hungry, Molly walked back to the edge of the river, and with her spoon caught up many little fishes. Some of the soldiers lit a fire and cooked them.

Molly fried the best herself for the princess, and all ate and enjoyed their dinner.

After this they started on the journey again. The princess was helped on to the white pony, and the sleeping soldier was secured on to the brown one. Thus, by slow degrees, they arrived at the gates of the town.

All the inhabitants rejoiced to see them, and welcomed them, some shouting and dancing

before them, whilst others threw flowers in
their path. On the steps of the palace stood
White-rose and Pink-rose ready to receive
them, and to their surprise the princesses were
not the least disappointed at seeing the old
woman ; but after thanking Fluffy and Molly
very warmly, they put their arms round their
sister, and kissing her over and over again,
they led her up into the hall. She seemed
very much touched by their love, and wept
with joy when they told her that there could
be no real difference so long as her heart was
as young as before. She assured them that it
was so, and smiled so sweetly on those that
stood around that it was quite evident she was
speaking the truth.

White-rose and Pink-rose then whispered
something to each other, and presently a little
page brought them a lovely wreath of red
roses laid on a cushion, and they placed it on
their old sister's head in the presence of every-
one. Scarcely had they done so, when she
became a beautiful little girl again. She was
even prettier than her sisters, for there was a

wonderful expression in her eyes, that had come since she had experienced so much.

Her sisters, and Fluffy and Molly, and all the soldiers, joined hands and danced round Red-rose. As they did so, they sang a song about "Love never really growing old," till at last, whilst they danced, the soldiers changed into children like the rest, and the sleepy one awoke, a child himself, too, and joined in the merry-making.

In the evening there were brilliant illuminations, and Fluffy and Molly stood hand in hand on the terrace of the palace garden, from which they could see them. They saw in the town below the inhabitants rejoicing, and dancing about with coloured lights and torches in their hands. Finally, there was a blaze of hundreds of rockets fired up into the air, higher than any that had been sent up before, and these words in red lights appeared :

"Princess Red-rose is saved,
thanks to
Fluffy the brave, and Molly the clever cook."

M

Then the princesses assured them they had succeeded in doing what few people ever do, for they had "realised their ideal."

Fluffy had never felt so happy in her life before, and she said :

"We have done a little, but I should like to do more still." Then she turned to Molly, saying. "Oh, hasn't it been nice? Isn't it grand? Wouldn't you like more adventures? Molly, Molly, why don't you answer?" and she shook Molly's hand, and opened her eyes wide, and found herself suddenly sitting on a bench in St. James's Park, and by her side sat a little workhouse child, holding her hand.

"You 'ave been calling of me, miss, ever so many times. But I must be off now, back to the workhouse, for I see the others have started already. Good-bye!"

"Good-bye, dear little Molly," said Fluffy regretfully; "but we shall meet again." And then she looked round and said to herself, "I know where I am quite well. Perhaps, if I run home, I shall overtake my brothers and sisters. Yes, there they are!"

And here the story ends. But perhaps some day you will meet Lady Fluffy or little Molly—both very useful people in their way—and if so, they will be able to tell you what happened next.

IV.

In the Track of the Snail.

In the attic of a wretched house overlooking
the Great Western Railway, there lived an old
woman, whose name was Mrs. Jarvis, and her
grandson, Richard Smith. Whenever fast
trains passed by everything in their room
shook and rattled, but they were quite used
to it, and did not mind the noise.

Dick was an orphan, and had it not been
for his grandmother he would have been sent
to the workhouse. But, though very poor,
she had brought him to her own home when
he was a few months old.

She paid for his schooling, and made all his
clothes, and often they had very little food to
eat, because she found difficulty in paying the
rent for their room, as all the money she had
to live on was what she could earn by needle-

"Dick took great pride in it."   [*Page* 181.

work, and this was not much. The room on the floor beneath them was larger, and their window opened on to the leads that covered part of it. This made a nice place where Dick could amuse himself in summer, and he fancied it was his garden. In one corner there was an old soap box, with the word "Sunlight" still visible on it. This was full of earth, and every summer a little musk and a few blades of grass grew up in it. Mrs. Jarvis had found the box when she came, and had encouraged the boy to water the flowers, and to consider it his own property. Dick took great pride in it, and was nearly as fond of the grass as of the flowers. There was a pot with mustard and cress next to it, which he used to cut and wash, and bring to his grandmother to eat at tea sometimes. She declared she had never tasted anything so good. The seed had been given to him, and he took great care of it, only sowing a very small quantity at a time.

Then there were about two dozen oyster shells that he liked to arrange and rearrange round the box and the flower-pot. For a time he would think the last arrangement was the best, until a new idea would come into his head, and then he altered them all again.

He kept also in another corner what he called his "tool box." It contained a knife, the blade of which was half broken, and he used it as a spade, with which to dig the earth over in the spring; an old comb, which was his rake; and a very old broom without a handle, with which he swept the whole of the leads. He had to kneel to do this, and always made himself very dirty with smuts.

In another corner, close to the window, was a barrel to catch the rain water off the roof. When he was quite little, his grandmother had often lifted him up to peep into this. Now he was too heavy for her to do so, but he had found, that by placing the tip of one foot in the wall, where a brick was fallen out, and by catching hold of the edge of the barrel, he could just look in. There was nothing to see, only black water; but still he liked looking, just because it was out of his reach.

His grandmother often took water out of it

to wash things with, as it was softer than what came from the tap ; but she shook her head over the dirt of it, and said, " Dear, dear ! How different from the water in Surrey ! " She had lived in that county as a child, but it was so long ago, she did not remember much about it now. Much as Dick asked her to describe to him what her home there had been, she could only remember that the water was clear, that she had lived in a cottage close to the high road, that there was a garden with a few flowers, whose names, however, she'd forgotten. At the age of fifteen she had come to London, and soon after had married a cabman. But, after some years, her husband was killed by an accident, and she had been left a widow with three children. Two had died before they grew up ; the third, a girl, Dick's mother, had married a glazier, but both she and her husband had died when he was a baby, and Mrs. Jarvis had taken care of him ever since. She had gone through many sorrows. She did not like to talk of sad things to Dick, so she said little about her former married life.

She hoped, when he grew up, he would take to some trade, and be an honest, useful man, and comfort her in her old age.

At present he did not feel inclined to choose a profession. Sometimes he thought he would like to be a soldier, sometimes a gardener, and sometimes a porter. However, he never said this to his grandmother, because she wished him to be a carpenter, plumber, or a glazier, and he felt sure he should never like any of these trades.

One summer evening, during the school holidays, he was playing silently on the leads. His grandmother had tied a line right across with all the washing hung on it to dry, and in spite of her telling him repeatedly that he was very much in the way, he assured her he would not move, or do any harm to the clothes, "Only don't speak, granny! I'm so very busy," and remained there still.

His business consisted in watching a snail that was crawling round the edge of the box of musk. He was very much interested, and did not know what it was, never having seen one before. He put his spade (the broken knife) in front of it, but the snail instantly withdrew into its shell. He then gently tapped the shell with his spade.

"Oh, please don't do that," it said. "Don't you know we snails feel through our shells? You did hurt me so!"

"I am sorry. Your shell looks quite hard, and I did not know it really belonged to you— I mean, that it was part of yourself."

"Of course it is! Just as much as your shell is part of yourself at present."

"My shell? I haven't got one!"

"Goosey! I mean your body is your shell. But I see you're not very old, and can't understand that yet. Please, will you tell me if I go straight on, where do I come to?"

"My name is not Goosey, it is Dick Smith."

"Well, Dick, will you tell me where I am going?"

"If you go on as you are doing, you will go round my garden and come back again to the same spot where you are now."

"Thanks. I am short-sighted and cannot see far; that's just the journey I wish to make to-night."

Dick laughed. "At the rate you seem to go, certainly it will take you a long time. But why not stop where you are, as you will only come back again?"

"Ah, you think I am slow? But time is nothing to me, for I live for ages. And though *slow*, I am *sure !* I intend going three times round this thing you call your garden, just as a solid beginning to a good end!"

"I don't understand at all," said Dick.

"Well, if you like to follow me you'll understand."

"Ha, ha, ha! Follow you, indeed! Why, I could hop round these leads on one leg a hundred times while you're crawling once round my garden!"

"Just try," was all the snail answered.

Dick forgot about the clothes, and began to hop; but the sleeve of one of his wet shirts, that hung on the line, flapped into his face, and the button hit him just in the eye, before it fell down. His grandmother called out to him to come in.

"I knew you'd knock something down. Come in directly, and bring in that shirt, it's dirty again now. You are tiresome to-day. I really begin to wish the holidays were over, and that you were back at school."

His eye hurt him, and he was sorry to have vexed his granny. He covered his face with his hand, and came to kiss her.

"I'm so sorry I knocked the shirt down, after you had washed it clean. I am a tiresome boy, but I do love you, so don't say you wish the holidays over."

"Well, well, you're a dear boy; never mind, I'm not really angry. What have you done to your eye? It's quite red."

"It will be all right soon, granny, if I keep it shut. It was the sleeve that flapped into my face."

He sat down on a stool beside her. His eye did hurt him for a few minutes.

"Who were you talking to?" she asked; and then added, "It's a bad trick to talk to one's self; it's common enough with old people, but for a child, it's queer."

"It was not to myself; it was to a creature that calls itself a snail," and then he told her all the conversation.

His grandmother smiled. "Perhaps it's a fairy; in any case it's best to be kind to any creature that's harmless, and I never heard of a snail hurting anything. We shall see," she added; "if it's a fairy there will be something unusual to be seen on your box to-morrow. Perhaps it will bring you good luck, who knows? At anyrate, we won't look to-night; it's dark, and time to go to bed now." She thought it all a joke, as she did not believe in fairies really.

Next morning, the moment Dick was up and awake, he ran to look out of the window in his night-shirt. No, there was nothing un-usual, as far as he could see. Of course, the snail might still be there, but he could not see that until he could dress and go out. How-ever, he had no time to look until after break-fast, for he always helped his grandmother with her housework in the morning before he amused himself.

It was very tiresome this morning that the kettle would not boil, and the bread would not toast; everything seemed to him very slow. "I believe," he said to himself, "it's the snail who is making everything so long and tiresome this morning."

At last, after breakfast, his grandmother fetched in the clothes, and said, laughing,

"Now you may go out. I'm sure you're longing to see your snail; but *I* can't see the creature anywhere, nor any luck either. I looked well on the leads for fear of crushing the poor thing, but there's nothing."

Dick did not answer, but ran out to his garden. It was true there was no snail, but there was something glistening round his garden. He touched it—it was a gold thread! He followed it with his finger, and it went three times round the box, and was fastened in a knot, just where he'd seen the snail the day before. He was delighted. After all, there was something unusual. He called out :

"Granny, granny, come quick and see what I've found!"

But the grandmother had gone out to carry the needlework she'd finished to her employer.

"She's gone out," he, said to himself; "but what's this? One end of the thread goes on, I see, from the knot, down the box, and along the leads."

He was flushed with excitement and pleasure. He crawled along to see where the thread went; he followed it in the gutter under the edge of the little wall, round the leads, right away to the barrel. Then he saw it went up the side, and over the edge, apparently, into the water.

"Oh, dear! can the poor little snail have fallen in and be drowned? Quick, quick! I must fetch the stool and look in."

When he came out with it he heard something splashing and mewing inside the barrel.

"That's the voice of a cat, and not a snail. Besides, it must be a much larger thing, to make such a splashing."

He put one foot on the stool, and the toe of

his other foot in the hole in the wall, and lifting himself by the top rim of the barrel, he could just see that it was half full of water, and a poor little kitten struggling about in it. He jumped down again, flung off his coat and waistcoat, climbed up, and let himself slide into the barrel, slowly, till his feet touched the bottom. The water was up to his shoulders, but he caught up the kitten by the nape of its neck, and saved it alive. Then he tried to climb out again, but this was impossible, for he was too little. He shouted for help, but for some minutes in vain. The water felt cold; he longed for his granny's return. At last he heard her come into the room, and he shouted with all his might:

"Granny, come and help me! I am in the water-butt, and I can't get out. Do come quickly, because my arm aches holding the kitten up."

The kitten was mewing also as loud as it could.

"Oh, my goodness gracious me! Bless the cat and all its kittens! How in the world did

you ever—did you ever—?   Well, to be sure !
Here, give me the creature," and she took it
from him.   When he had both his hands free,
he managed, with some difficulty, to climb out,
but when he appeared, she exclaimed : " What
a mess !   Oh, what a *filthy boy !*   Talk of
Pears !   Why, it would take that, and Brooke's,
Hudson's, Sunlight, Vinolia, Ivy, and the
whole lot of them, to get you clean again !
Deary, deary me !   Couldn't you have fished
the kitten out with the coal-scuttle, or dust-pan,
or shovel, for all the world, without getting in
with your whole body, and half drowning of
yourself?   Ough !   It will take me half a day,
with a dozen scrubbing brushes, mops, towels,
and dusters, to get you clean and dry again,
and a fortnight's washing of your things after
that ; and then, I suppose, it will be time again
for you to be trying some new pranks !   Indeed, indeed, I don't know what to do with
you !   My belief is, you're old enough to be
learning some trade.   Then you'd not have
time to be splashing and playing in the water-
barrel."

" But, granny, I wasn't playing. You would not have wished me to let the kitten drown before my eyes without trying to save it ? "

His grandmother only muttered something about kittens, and grandchild, and dirt, and bother, and worry, and work, and toiling, and moiling, as she stepped back into the room, holding the kitten still. She was very angry, but it did not last long. She washed the animal and wiped it dry, and was pleased to see it was really a very pretty tortoise-shell kitten. As to Dick's clothes, she found they were not so much spoilt as she had thought. She even said he was a good boy to have taken off his coat and waistcoat, and by dinner-time she was quite the kind old granny again that Dick loved.

However, after dinner, when he had time to think, he sat on the leads near the musk, and began to consider what he ought to do. Soon he would have passed the fifth standard—he was quick for his age—then he would be a soldier or a porter. A soldier, he thought, would be the best, but then he might not be

N

able to look after his granny.   Perhaps the
snail might give him some advice, as it certainly was something uncommon, for it was
able to speak, and had tied such a pretty gold
thread round his box.   That reminded him,
where did the thread end?   He'd been so
occupied in saving the kitten, he'd forgotten to
look for the thread.   He went to the barrel
again, and there it was, hanging over the edge,
so he pulled it gently, very gently, and up
came the end, and nothing more.

"I wonder if snails can live in the water?
I'll just speak to it, and perhaps it will
answer."

He climbed up again and first whispered, but
when there was no answer, he shouted, "Mr.
Snail, are you there?"

But there was no sound in answer.   He
took the end of the thread and rolled it carefully up, and laid it beside his garden.   Then
the kitten came out on the leads, and they
played together.   He talked to it, but it was
only a common kitten; it did not seem to
understand, and could not speak.   His grand-

mother allowed him to keep the animal, and many months went by, and nothing particular occurred.

He went to school again, and soon passed the fifth standard. His granny said she should apprentice him now to a glazier whom she knew, but he begged her to allow him just a week's holiday before settling anything.

He had looked daily to see if the thread was just where he put it ; and it lay rolled up just the same, only it never seemed to get dirty, which Dick thought a good sign.

"It must be something peculiar, for everything in London gets soil'd in a minute. It may bring me luck yet!" So he left it where it was.

Of course he was too old now to play with his garden beyond just watering it like a grown-up person. The oyster shells lay just as he had arranged them before he'd seen the snail. He was still fond of the leads, but he felt it was no longer the whole world for him.

Every day of that week before he was

apprenticed he wandered about the streets to
see if any tradesman had a notice written up,
"Wanted a Boy." For he thought the life
of an errand boy would be better fun than
a glazier's, and he was not near old enough
to be a porter.

However, he saw nothing to suit him till the
very last day of the week that his granny had
allowed him, and then he saw at the window
of a smart bonnet shop, "Wanted a Boy."
So he inquired, and Mrs. Hollyhock, the
milliner, was pleased with his appearance.
She said, provided his grandmother would
consent, and that the schoolmaster spoke well
of him, she would engage him for a few
shillings a week.

His grandmother consented, for she found,
after all, it would cost too much to apprentice
him to the glazier, as she had at first resolved
to do.

All went well. He carried bonnet boxes to
different houses, and Mrs. Hollyhock was
satisfied. He seemed quick and intelligent,
and later on she trusted him to take boxes,

and wait for the money. He brought back the money, and could always remember exactly who had not paid ; and the bills were always brought back clean. So altogether Mrs. Hollyhock was pleased.

However, one day a misfortune happened. He was to take a bandbox full of artificial flowers, for a lady to choose those she wished to have. She was a very long time about it, but at last she took two sprays, and he was able to leave the house again with the remainder. It was getting dark, and rather foggy. He hurried along through the streets, but, before he got to Mrs. Hollyhock's shop, he saw, at the door of a public-house, a big boy roughly push a very little girl out of his way, and, in doing so, knock the basket she was carrying into the gutter. She was bruised and hurt, and cried. Dick stopped, for he felt very sorry for her. The big boy was out of sight in a moment, or he might have ventured to cuff him, for he was brave enough for that. It may have been lucky he did not get the chance, for it would have been difficult to prove who was in the right, as no policeman was present. Dick put down his bandbox, and picked up the girl's basket, which had been full of eggs, but they were all smashed and in a mess now.

"Oh, my stepmother will whip me so, and it was not my fault! It was that wicked, horrid boy! He's always getting me into trouble!" the girl exclaimed.

"Do you know him, then?" asked Dick.

"Yes; he's my stepmother's son. She says he's my brother, but he's not! He's not a brother, for he's so unkind. Oh, dear! I'm so *miserable!*" and she cried again.

"How many eggs had you?"

Between gulps and sobs she answered:

"A whole shilling's worth! and I shall get thrashed once for every single penny! Oh, dear! oh, dear! I daren't go home!"

Dick felt in his pockets. He had a ten shilling piece, and half-a-crown; but that was Mrs. Hollyhock's money. He had a sixpenny bit; but he was taking it to his granny, for it was part of his wages. There were also

three pennies; those were his very own.
He thought a minute. If he gave her ninepence, the little girl might buy more eggs,
and only get whipped three times. But then,
his granny was very, very poor! Was it
wrong towards her? Tears came into his own
eyes, because he pitied the little girl, and yet
he was not sure how to do right. Then
suddenly he took the sixpenny bit.

"There, little girl," he said, "take that. I
am sorry I can't make it ninepence."

She began to thank him, but Dick had
turned to pick up his bandbox, and it was
gone! Crowds of people were passing. It
was stupid to have let go his box even for a
minute in this street.

"Oh, what a fool I was! My box is gone!
It's stolen! What shall I do?"

The little girl was thanking him, but he did
not listen. He hastened on. He must tell
Mrs. Hollyhock what had happened. She
would be sure to send him away. He would
then earn nothing. It was all wretched.

Mrs. Hollyhock was out when he arrived.

He gave up the money and bill to the fore-woman, and said:

" I'll come in the morning and explain about the flowers."

" Did the lady, then, keep them all? "

" I'll explain in the morning to Mrs. Holly-hock herself.   Good-night."

She muttered something about " cheeky boy," and shut the door in his face.

He felt relieved.   At least, now, he would have some hours to think over his misfortune. When he came home he gave his threepence to his granny, saying :

" It ought to be sixpence, but I gave that to a child, and this is what you gave me for my own."

She looked at him as he laid it on her lap, and she saw he was very pale, and his lips trembled as if he was very much agitated.

" Dick, tell me—something has happened—tell me quickly.   You have surely done nothing wrong?"

Then he burst into tears, and flinging him-self on the ground at her feet, he told her all that had happened, and, sobbing his heart out, he buried his head in her lap. She tried to comfort him.

" Dick, my darling boy, don't cry so ; you'll break my heart. Dear child, don't cry. Why, it might be much worse. There's nothing wrong in what you've done, only a mistake putting down that box—and all to do good to the child. Well, deary, maybe Mrs. Hollyhock will believe you, and you can keep on giving back half your wages till you've paid for those flowers. I'll manage very well. I'll work an hour more in the evening, I will."

But this made Dick cry afresh.

"Granny, that's just it. You're always slaving away, and it's *I* who ought to be keeping *you* now. You ought not to be working so hard any more."

" Well, my darling, you'll grow up soon and earn a good deal of money, and I'll be a lady then, and do nothing but sit with a black silk apron on, and only knit your socks. There now, my boy, don't—don't be so unhappy."

She got up and put the supper ready. The

kitten, who was nearly a cat now, purred, and came and rubbed himself against Dick, and tried to comfort him.

The old woman and the boy sat down, and each tried to eat, but the food seemed to choke them ; so, after pretending for some time to each other that they were enjoying their food, they gave it up, and said it was bedtime, and retired to rest.

Mrs. Jarvis could see, from her bed, the trains as they passed. For hours she lay watching them. The express passed like a flash of lightning. Some trains came into the town slowly, puffing and snorting by fits and starts, and stood just under the house; then, with groans, and creaks, and shrill whistles, they moved on a hundred yards, and stopped again. Her life, she thought, was like these luggage trains. She and her grandchild had got on so slowly ; now and then poverty had threatened to stop them altogether ; then for a short time Dick had earned a few shillings a week, and all seemed to promise well. Now this misfortune had happened, and all because of her boy's kind heart. It was very, very hard, she thought, and though she had tried to cheer him with the idea that Mrs. Hollyhock would still keep him if he promised to repay her, she had not really thought it likely. She feared, on the contrary, that there would be very unpleasant things for her and Dick next day. She went on thinking and thinking, and only fell asleep early in the morning.

Dick had cried so much that his pillow was wet, and so was the sheet all round his poor little face, because he had wiped his eyes on it. However, he had slept very soon, and woke up only at the usual time next day. For the first moment he had forgotten everything, and yet he felt there was something horrid he had got to do.

"Ah, yes, now I remember, I must go to Mrs. Hollyhock and tell her the box of flowers was stolen—how dreadful! but I had better get it over quickly."

He dressed himself, and moved about softly not to wake up his granny. Then he peeped out of the window to see if it was still foggy.

No, it was a bright day, but rather cold. Luckily they had a little fuel and food, enough to last two days ; but after that he feared there would be nothing but the threepence to buy anything with, if, as he was afraid, Mrs. Hollyhock turned him away.   Perhaps she would have him put in prison, if he could not prove his innocence!   How dreadful!   At this moment his eyes happened to fall on the steps leading to the leads.   There was the gold thread!   He was very much surprised ; he had quite forgotten the snail ; perhaps it had come again!   He opened the window, slipped out, and closed it after him, for he was afraid his granny would feel the cold air.   He ran first to his garden to see if the thread was rolled up as he left it.   No—it was gone—but it was pulled tight from the knot round the box, and went straight to the water butt! There it seemed to go up, and over the top, down again, and then under the window into the room.   He had grown older and taller, so that when he stood on tiptoe he could look into the barrel.   That is what he did now, and

saw to his great delight and joy—what?
Why! the whole of it was full of beautiful,
artificial flowers! Enough to fill a dozen and
more boxes like the one he had lost! He
thought, "How funny! And where is the
water?" The whole barrel was carefully
lined with tissue paper. He was so surprised
that he stood for some minutes with his mouth
and eyes wide open. Then he considered it
would be best to take some flowers quickly to
Mrs. Hollyhock, and just say, "Here are some
flowers like those I lost; I'm sorry I've not got
a box, but I've brought these in paper." Yes,
yes! He would do this before his breakfast,
and before his granny woke. What fun! what
fun! and on his return he'd explain all
to her. She might sell the other flowers, and
have money enough soon "to sit like a lady
and do nothing"! (He had not yet seen much
of the world, so he thought that ladies did
nothing.)

He promptly snatched out two pieces of the
tissue paper, picked out the flowers he remembered the box contained: six poppies, three

sprays of lilac, a bunch of roses, a bunch of
violets, a spray of daisies and grass—that was
all.   Then he slipped softly through the room,
catching up his cap as he passed, and ran as
fast as he could to Mrs. Hollyhock.   Tap-tap,
he knocked at her door, and she opened it
herself.

"Oh! I thought you were the milkman!"
she exclaimed; "how early you are to-day.
Those are the flowers, yes, I see, quite right!
The box got smashed? well, never mind,
you're a good boy! and I shall raise your
wages in another three months."   She did not
give him time to explain, but felt sure she
knew everything, and liked to have all the
talking to herself.   He thanked her, and she
gave her orders hurriedly.   "You can run
home now, I sha'n't want you till twelve
o'clock; then you'll have to carry the brides-
maids' hats I'm just finishing to the different
houses.   There are eight of them, and only
two are sisters living in the same house, so
you'll have to look sharp, for I promised they
should all have them to-day."

After this last sentence she banged the door, not because she was cross, but because she wanted to get back to her work quickly. Dick ran home, and found his granny had prepared breakfast, but had not begun to eat yet. She was sitting over the fire with her work-box on her lap, unrolling something it contained. He now noticed the gold thread reached from the window into the old woman's work. He had been so overjoyed at finding the flowers, he had forgotten to see where the thread went to after that. Mrs. Jarvis shook her head over the parcel she was undoing, and said :

" I do believe, Dick, you're up to some trick this morning. Surely you were not deceiving me last night when you said you'd lost the box of flowers ? See here, there's—a something— I do believe it's a present—from you ? But how could you buy anything when you've no money ? Look here," and she shook it free from the paper that was wrapped round it, " I do believe it's a black silk apron. Oh, my! how beautiful! But, Dick—how did you get it ? " and she looked at him over her spectacles and added, " Oh, Dick, is it all right ?   What is the meaning of it ? "

" I know nothing whatever about it, granny ; but it must be a fairy, or that snail I told you of long ago, because there is his gold thread," and he pointed it out to her ; but it was so fine she had to stare fixedly through her spectacles before she could make it out at all.

Then he told her about the water-barrel being full of flowers, and throwing a shawl right over her head, she went out with him to look.

" Why, Dick, there's enough to keep a shop !   How queer !   How extraordinary ! Well, I never ! "

They sat down to breakfast after that, and they both declared they were at that moment "the merriest, happiest two people in London."

It was settled that Mrs. Jarvis should take a few of the flowers in a basket every day and sell them to some bonnet-maker, but not to Mrs. Hollyhock, because they did not wish to be questioned.   In the meantime, they carefully took them all out of the barrel, and put them in a trunk in their room. The old woman sold some wallflowers and yellow roses that very day, and bought provisions with the money. In the evening, when Dick returned, he found the supper ready, and his granny sitting before the fire, with her hands folded on her new silk apron, doing nothing.

"Darling boy," she said, "I thought it would please you to find me doing nothing."

"Yes, granny, I am delighted to see you like a lady."

"Yes, but to-morrow you'll find me knitting, because it is no happiness to me to be idle. Also, I'm sure, if it is a fairy who has helped us, it will be displeased if we don't try to help ourselves."

"Oh, yes," said Dick, "I intend getting on and earning money, and when I am old enough I think I shall try to be a porter at Paddington. I've always had a fancy for that." And after a pause he added, "Later on, I might rise to something higher, granny—I *might* be made a stationmaster."

Here his granny nearly choked with laughter, as she was eating some toast, and a crumb got down her throat the wrong way. She coughed, and at last, wiping the tears from her eyes, she exclaimed:

"*You* a stationmaster! Why, you'd forget the time the trains were due, and there would be a grand smash of expresses, engines, and luggage trains, all running into each other. Oh, there would be a fine to-do! No, indeed! A porter, yes, that may be; but a station-master! Well, if you were at a station in a wilderness, with just one train running in the day, perhaps then you would remember it. But, oh, dear, you do make me laugh!"

"Well, granny, laugh. I like to hear you; but for all that I mean to try. Think how lucky I've been so far. Mrs. Hollyhock is going to pay me more money in three months."

"You're right, Dick, you've a great deal to be thankful for, and so have I. I am thankful," she added softly, "to have such a good grandson, for you are a dear boy," and she got up to clear away the supper things, and gave him a hearty kiss. "Only to think how we both cried last night, and this evening we are laughing as gay as gay."

Dick suddenly said :

" By the by, what did you do with the gold thread ? "

" I rolled it up tight, and let it rest near the window."

He went to look, and there it was.

" I often wonder where the snail has gone to," he thought to himself, when later, tired out, he lay down to sleep.

Now, two or three years passed, and nothing particular happened. Dick had left Mrs. Hollyhock with a very good character, and he was now a porter on the railway. His granny had taken great care of the money he earned ; she had been able to put a little in the savings' bank. They rented two rooms now, but one was the same. Dick had many boxes of flowers on the leads, and was still very fond of "his property," although he had very little time for sitting there now. At his work he was reckoned quick and intelligent. He still had a kind heart, and showed it by being gentle and helpful to children and aged people who got in or out of the trains, and also to poor animals who were packed up very uncomfortably for travelling. Sometimes he was on night duty, but generally he worked during the day.

One evening, as he came home very tired indeed (for it was a bank holiday, and therefore there had been extra hard work on account of the excursion trains), he said good-night to his granny, and was going to tumble into bed, when he remembered he had not watered his flowers. It was a hot summer's night, with many stars shining brightly. He could see to water them quite well. When he had dipped the can into the barrel to fill it with water, and carried it to the box of musk, which he always watered first, he saw the gold thread was moved. Ever since the artificial flowers had appeared, he had left the end rolled up just inside the window. Now he saw that it went from the knot on the box over the edge of the roof, and disappeared down, down the wall of the room underneath. He felt it with his hand as far as he could reach.

" Now, this is something unusual," he said to himself ; " the snail or the fairy has been here. Tired as I am, I must follow it."

But how ? That was the next question. He could not trust to the gold thread to let himself down by. " It's strong enough for a snail, but not for a man," he thought. After a moment's consideration he lit a lantern, and, running downstairs softly, he unfastened the back door that opened into a small court about four yards square, on the same side of the house as his garden was. He turned to the right to look on the wall, and there, true enough, hung the thread, and he saw that it went along the yard and over the outer wall near the railway lines. The wall was not high. He climbed over, and let himself drop on to the ground. " Higher than I thought," he said, when he came down on his feet with such a shock that it shook him all over, and made his jaw ache, and put out his lantern. But there was no mistake, for when he had struck a light, he saw he was following the thread all right. It lay along beside the rails towards the west, towards the country.

He held the lantern in front and ran along as fast as he could. An express train dashed past him ; he had only just time to step out of the way ; the wind it made rushing past blew out his lantern once more. Again he lit it and ran on half a mile. " I shall find the snail this time, for he's made the thread ever so much longer, I shall catch him at it now."

He'd scarcely said this before he came to a signal-box, on the steps of which there was the end of the thread and the snail. Dick knelt and whispered :

" Oh, my dear friend, I am glad to find you at last. Now I can thank you for your kind—"

" Hush ! Don't waste time," the snail interrupted him, " run up quick and pull the signal. The fifth handle to the right as you enter. Quickly, I say ! The train, the train ! "

In the distance two red eyes were coming

along the line straight in front. Dick hesitated no longer, but ran up, burst into the little room, rushed to the fifth handle on the right, and pulled it. When the express came by, he could hear the engine-driver shouting out something very angrily; but he also heard them putting on the drags, and then several shrill whistles, and the train stopped about a quarter of a mile further on.

Then he turned to see what the signalman was about. He saw the poor fellow lying on the ground quite pale, as if he were dead, but on coming nearer he saw the man was still breathing. He had wounded his hand badly, evidently whilst cutting a piece of bread which lay by his side, and then had fainted right away. Some vein was bleeding. Dick understood at once. He rolled up his necktie as a pad and placed it on the wound, then he tore off a strip of his own shirt, and bandaged the man's hand up tight, holding it up the while to prevent it bleeding.

Glancing round the room he saw there was nothing to give him but water. A few drops of this he let trickle in the man's mouth, and it seemed to do him good.   He rolled up his own coat as a cushion for the man's head as he lay on the floor.   When he had done all this the snail appeared on the top step.

" You're a capital boy, Dick," it said.

" A *man*, you mean," he answered, smiling, and stooping down to his friend.

" Dick, your a brick !   But now, write down what I tell you, for you will have to attend to ·the signals for some hours yet."

" I wish I could give the man something to drink.   He'll die if help does not come soon."

The snail did not answer, but twisting the gold thread once round the leg of the table, it crawled up to the keyhole of a cupboard in the wall.

"Goosey, don't you see some broth in there ? "

Dick opened it, and saw a jug of cold broth. He heated it over the gas that was burning in the room, and gave some to the man, who now began to revive a little and open his eyes for a minute, but was too weak to speak. The snail exclaimed :

· "Quick! Pull the third handle to the left; there are luggage trucks coming in the way of the London midnight train."

Dick instantly did as he was told. Then he carefully wrote down the different trains expected, and what signals to put up, and when to pull them down again. The snail explained everything very clearly, and then said :

" Now I shall leave you, for I've many other people to help besides you. At five in the morning the other signalman will come to your relief."

" Oh, thank you, a hundred times thank you! You are a kind fair—" he did not finish his thanks, for the snail vanished.

For the next few hours, Dick walked up and down the small room. He did not dare sit down for fear of falling asleep, but he felt very weary, and longed, and longed, to be relieved. He watched the clock and attended to the signals. Every half hour he let a little soup trickle down the man's throat, and often anxiously looked at the wounded hand. The arm lay, raised on a bundle of old sacking he had found, to keep the limb from bleeding. It seemed no worse; on the contrary, the man appeared rather better, and glad to swallow the soup.

At four o'clock he turned out the gas. There was a beautiful sunrise that shone through the glass walls of the room, and filled it with pink and gold light. On the window ledge there stood a box with musk, and another with mignonette. It reminded him of his own; he watered the flowers, for the earth felt dry.

"It's lucky all this happened on such a lovely summer's night. Had it been winter," he said to himself, "I'm sure this poor fellow would have died, and I doubt if I could have held out all these hours."

At four thirty-five he put up the last signal written on the paper. He felt dreadfully drowsy; indeed, he fell asleep for a few minutes, and woke up with a start as a man stepped into the open door, exclaiming:

" Hulloa ! What's happened ? "

Then Dick shook himself together, and told him about the man's state, and how he'd managed all the signals,

" You must be an awfully clever chap to know the signals without learning them. I suppose he told you ? " he asked, pointing to the sick man, but not waiting for an answer; glancing at the clock he rushed to a signal and pushed it. Then he went on, " Well, it's all very lucky; but how did you know Sam was hurt ? "

" That would take too long to explain. Tell me where I can get help for him ? "

" Oh, I'll manage that. I can telegraph to the next signal-box, where there are two men. I'll soon get him carried away."

" All right," said Dick, snatching up the end of the gold thread, and winding it round his fingers.

He went on doing this all the time as he walked home until he reached the wall of his house. Here he stopped to secure the thread into a knotted ball, and left it hanging there.

He could not return over the wall, for on this side it was far too high. He had a few minutes' walk to the station, and so round to his home. The landlady was up and let him in.

"Don't ask me questions, I'm dead beat, I must sleep a few hours," he said, as he hurried past her upstairs.

She stared at him, and thought he looked haggard, worn, and odd.

"Perhaps he's drunk; but if so it's very strange, for he's such a steady lad," and then she went about her business.

In the meantime, Dick tottered into his room and out on to the leads.

"I must put by the thread, or my luck is gone." So, with his eyes half shut, he pulled and he pulled.

He felt it come for a yard or two, and then it stuck.

"Well, it's safe out of the way of people walking under the wall, there it must remain for the present."

Then he went in, and flung himself on his

bed just as he was, and slept soundly for some hours. At last he woke up, for he felt something scratching his face, and, opening his eyes wide, he found the cat was sitting on his chest.

"Oh, pussy, what a bore you are; I've not slept near enough."

"Not enough!" exclaimed Mrs. Jarvis, as she came in. "Why, do you know you ought to have been at work half-an-hour ago? Here's some hot coffee I've brought you. I've been to look at you before, but I thought you seemed tired, and with your clothes all on, too. I could not understand it. You weren't so late as all that last night. Perhaps it's those excursion trains yesterday? Bank holiday, indeed! We hadn't such things when I was young."

"Where's my coat, granny? I must be off; it's late."

She looked about.

"I can't find it, and look at your arm. Whatever have you done to your shirt? Why, it's torn as if you'd been playing with lions and tigers. Is it that cat, think you?."

"Oh, I remember now, granny, I've had a night of adventure; but no time to tell you now. Give me another shirt, please."

He hastily dressed, putting on his Sunday coat, and went to the station, and began to apologise to one of the inspectors.

"All right, my man, I've heard all about it. Splendid! It's all owing to you that express last night did not get smashed up into splinters, and hundreds of people weren't killed. I say, you are a clever chap. Who taught you?"

"A friend—a—" he murmured.

"Well, look sharp, your coat is in the office; it was by that we knew *you* had been in the signal-box, and done it all. Come quickly back, for we want you to work as usual for a time till the company give you something better. There, don't stare like a stuck pig," he added, as Dick stood with his mouth wide open, which was one of the boyish tricks he never could cure himself of.

There was no more talking that day. He had luggage to wheel about, and to answer nervous old ladies, who, if they hadn't lost a bag or a box, were frightened lest they should lose the train. He tried to be civil, and do his duty as usual; but all the time there seemed a little song in his ears. "Splendid! Saved hundreds of lives! Something better—something! Hundreds of lives saved!"

In the evening, just as he was leaving off work, the stationmaster said:

"Perhaps you'll hear from the company tomorrow; I congratulate you."

Dick bowed his thanks, but could not speak, he felt too happy.

He told everything to his granny when he came home, and she was silent from surprise at the news. She felt inclined to cry with pride and happiness. She threw her arms round him at last, and said:

"My boy! my dear Dick! my darling! I'm so happy!"

Next morning he remembered the thread, and determined to finish pulling it up and putting it by. After watering his flowers he took hold of the end of it that was tied to his box and pulled. This time it did not seem

to be caught. It came easily; but it felt as
if something was hanging to it; and Dick
thought the "something" was heavier than
the ball of thread itself would be.

"No doubt it's a bit of ivy off the top of
the wall, or a scrap of rubbish of some kind
that has got entangled in it."

He leant over the edge, but he could not
see. However, his attention was attracted by
a voice saying :

"Steady now! Don't be in too great a
hurry."

"It's the snail!" he exclaimed. "But it's
not he alone who makes the difference in the
weight." Then he leant over and whispered :
"All right! I'm so glad I shall have a chance
of thanking you."

"Oh, steady, steady! the thread is twisting
so! I shall be so giddy," said the voice.

He stretched out his hand as far as he
could reach to steady the thread, and drew
it up gently. Suddenly he felt he'd caught
a bit of cloth lined with something stiff in his
hand. Before he could guess what it was, he

lifted it over the edge and saw a station-master's cap, with a thick gold band round it, and in small letters embroidered in gold, " G.W.R." Also on the rim was the snail.

Where was the ball of thread? It was *all embroidered* round the cap, and was the smartest Dick had ever seen.

" Has your post come in yet?" asked the snail.

" No," answered Dick.

" Well, this cap will be useful to you. After you get your letters you'll under-stand."

" Dear snail, is it a fairy's gift you've brought me ? "

" Yes, yes, of course ! You don't suppose I'm an every-day sort of snail, do you ? Nor is the cap a common one, either. You'll soon find out that, without it, you cannot get on at all."

" And—and—"

Dick hesitated, as if he wanted to ask some-thing.

" Well, out with it ! What ? "

P

"And to whom, or to what, do I owe this great gift?"

"To your kindness to children, to the aged, and to animals! I was often invisible while you were at work, and watched you, Dick. I've seen you give water to pigeons arriving in hampers at the station. I've heard you speaking kindly to dogs, also, that were chained together, labelled, and miserable. A hundred little tiny things like that, nothing in themselves, only something when gathered up in a lump; and that is what *I* have done. I am a fairy, as you have guessed. The queen of the London fairies has commanded me to look after all the 'kind little nothings.' That is my work, and I do what I can."

"But," said Dick, "I don't remember—"

"No, very likely you've forgotten them. Well, none of the *kind little nothings* are lost! But they are as well forgotten, or conceit would come and spoil all. Good-bye! Remember you're nothing without the cap."

"Oh, don't go! Dear snail, explain to me, do, what—"

But the snail was transformed into a small fairy ; the shell was suddenly divided in two, and became wings glistening like opals on his shoulders. He flew up in the air, and hovered for a minute in front of Dick's astonished gaze, and then—there was nothing—he vanished.

When Dick recovered from his surprise, he wound the short piece of thread that remained round the box of musk, and went in holding his cap in his hand.

His granny had prepared breakfast, and held up a long blue envelope.

" Here, my boy, here's a letter."

He tore it open, and read out to his granny the contents. It was all written in very grand words to say that Richard Smith, for his prompt and intelligent action on such and such a night, would receive the unusual reward of being appointed stationmaster at Snail-Shell station, some miles from London, on the Great Western line.

" Oh," he exclaimed, " this is more than I deserve ! And shall I be clever enough ? " Then suddenly he remembered the cap he still held in his hand; he put it on, and, to his great surprise, he felt very clever indeed. He snatched up a pen and a sheet of notepaper, and wrote his thanks, and then read it aloud to his granny.

She clapped her hands together, and said, " That's very well put, and you do look wise with that cap on ! "

Then they ate their breakfast in silence, for they both wished to think over all that had happened.

Before leaving London, they had to sell some of their furniture, and arrange what things to take to their new home; but the days went by quickly. Whenever Dick was in doubt as to what was right or wise to do, he clapped on his cap, and instantly knew, and did it.

They took away with them the old box full of musk (with the short piece of gold thread still tied round), the broken knife and comb, the old broom, and also the water-barrel. The neighbours laughed, but they did not care; they said, " These old things are keepsakes, and remind us of—of the past." It was no use explaining more to them.

Years passed, and Dick was reckoned a very good stationmaster, whose orders were given promptly and wisely. He never grew conceited if people thought him clever, because he knew it was only owing to his never taking off his cap. He always kept it on when he was on duty; he never lifted it to bow even; he preferred touching it in military fashion, for fear of losing the fairy gift. Only on Sundays, or during hours of rest, he took it off, and sat with his granny in their sitting-room. They loved to talk over all that had happened when they were together. His granny would sit with her black silk apron on, stroking the cat, who lay on her lap the while, and sometimes she would exclaim, " I am so thankful—well, to be sure—you, Dick, a stationmaster! Well, I never! Who would have thought it?" And this is the end of the story.

V.

The Fairies' Dispute.

It was a beautiful summer evening in July,
when most people in London had done working, and those who were not too tired were
walking or sitting in the parks and gardens,
enjoying the cooler air after a very hot day.
There was a peculiar bright yellow light all
over the sky, which made the poor and the
rich rejoice together in the same thought—the
thought that there was going to be a spell of
lovely weather! No fogs, no rain, and
although it was a little too hot, yet that was
better than a cold, rainy July, which, when it
comes, makes people feel as if there had been
no summer at all.

This particular evening, two fairy queens
had agreed to meet on Westminster Bridge.
When the Tower clock struck eight, there was

"The leaves made nice, soft chairs for them to sit on."   [*Page* 231.

soft music in the air, and a fluttering of wings, and the two queens sat down, side by side, on a flower-seller's little cart, that was passing at the time. It was just the thing to suit fairies, as this donkey-cart was full of beautiful flowers, palms, and ferns, and the leaves made nice, soft chairs for them to sit on.

Now, one was a country fairy and the other was a London fairy. They were both very busy, and did not often meet; but this evening they had arranged to have a long talk quietly together. Their conversation lasted a long time. The man who led the cart often stopped to sell his flowers on his way home; though he did not know what distinguished company he was driving, he found that he was now selling more than he had sold all day, for of course the presence of such fairies brought him good luck.

This good fortune lasted, however, only until he sold the very plants the fairies were on. These were bought by a hospital nurse, who was on her way home.

She was a lady who had taken to nursing

because she loved it. Just now she was very much interested in a poor young woman in her ward at the hospital, who she believed was dying slowly. She bought these flowers with her own money to give to the woman. But she neither saw the fairies, nor heard them, as she hurried along with the flowers ; yet they were talking very loud (at least, as loud as fairies ever talk), because they were quarrelling. They were disputing and arguing so much that they never noticed they were no longer in the cart.

At last the country fairy, who was the least excitable of the two, said :

· "Don't let us really get angry, for it would be sad if you and I, who have known each other so many years, should not be able to settle this little difference amicably."

"You are so obstinate in your opinion," said the London fairy ; " you won't allow me to explain that—"

"Yes, yes ; but I have calmly tried to convince you that I've found in the country, in a lovely garden—" said the other, but was interrupted again.

"Oh, hush! Don't go on repeating yourself! I know what you've said, but it does not convince me. The long and short of it is, that you say you have found a beautiful, pure, excellent thing, in the country, and that you defy me to find anything to equal it in London. Now, I say, stuff and nonsense! I'm sure I can, only I have not searched about yet. I have not so much time as you; besides, I have not thought about it!"

"Well, don't let us quarrel. Supposing you come to-night with me and see what I mean? I can show it you, and then you will admit that you cannot find anything so pure, so good, and so lovely, born or growing, in London. Mind you! there may be some like it brought into this town, but they all come from the country."

The London fairy looked annoyed; but after a moment's thought she said:

"Well, I'll come; but wait until this nurse has carried us indoors. I'm tired of talking. Sit quiet here with me."

" Dear me ! We're no longer on the cart. I never noticed it before."

"Hush!" said the other. "Do let us be still and rest!"

It was not long before the nurse entered the hospital, and placed the flower-pot in her own room.

"To-morrow I'll give it to her," she said. "To-night she's probably dozing."

The fairies, like all fairies, were very in-quisitive; so they signed to each other, and one sat on the nurse's right shoulder and the other on the left, and went thus with her into the ward. The other nurses came forward and whispered :

"While you were out, the woman was suddenly much worse; she won't know you, we fear." But as she approached the invalid, a smile of recognition appeared on her pale face.

"Dear nurse," she faintly whispered, "I'm dying. Oh, my child! my Lily! If I only knew where she is!"

The nurse bent over her, trying to comfort her.

"You've prayed for your child. You've done all you can."

"Yes," she answered, "all I could do I've done. I've tried to forgive her father for taking her away from me. I hope if she's not with good people she will die, and then she will meet me in heaven."

The last words were said so softly, only the nurse could hear them.

When she had passed away the fairies were sad and thoughtful, and flew out of the window together.

"I wish I could find that child," said the London fairy.

"It will be difficult, dear sister," said the other, "for this city is swarming with people. But come! you've promised to let me show you my treasure."

They now spread out their gossamer wings very wide, and flew rapidly through the air for miles and miles. The moon shone brightly, and all the stars were come out, when the country fairy stopped on the top of a garden wall.

" See there!" she said, and pointed to a beautiful white flower growing straight up, out of a bed of mignonette. There were three large flowers on one stalk. The heart was yellow, but all the rest of the flower was pure white, and scented the night air with a strong, sweet smell, stronger than the mignonette.

The London fairy sighed and flew down, and laid her cheek on the side of one of the flowers.

" Oh, how lovely! how sweet! how clean! No, I have not seen so pure a thing in London. It could not grow; it would be choked in the smoke. Do give it me!"

" Yes," said the other fairy, " I might do so. It's growing unobserved here, where no one lives. The gardener has died, and the owner of this place is far away, travelling in the East. It certainly is wasted here, but I will not pluck it until you can find its equal in town!" adding, with a triumphant smile, " How long will it take you to do so, sister?"

Two tears came into the other one's eyes.

" It is not kind to talk thus. You know it

is so difficult to find, and therefore you promise to pick this flower when I have done so. Can't you be generous and give it me to-night? Oh, do! and I'll acknowledge I have nothing like it in London. I humbly ask you to give this to me, and let me fly away with it now."

"No, no! You said you were sure you could find something to equal it. Find it, sister! In any form—I am not particular as to its shape; only remember it must be as beautiful and pure. How many days, now, will you have to seek it?"

The London fairy did not answer, but stood gazing at the flower. Suddenly a thought seemed to have come to her, and she answered more cheerily:

"If such a thing exists, I'll find it before to-morrow night. You said it matters not as to its nature or form? Well, by to-morrow night I promise to tell you whether there is no such treasure in my kingom. Where shall we meet?"

"On the top of St. Paul's, at midnight, to-morrow."

"Agreed, then! Good-bye till to-morrow."
And the London fairy vanished.

The country fairy rolled herself up in a very
large dock-leaf that grew in this deserted
garden, and slept as country fairies usually
do. Not so the London fairy! When she
came back to her home in London (a secret
place, that human beings know nothing of), she
called out to all her subjects—the fairies "Ha-
ha!" and "No, nò!" and "Cheeky," and
"Peradventure," and many, many others.
She called them all by their names, and they
came, rubbing their eyes, for they had been
all fast asleep.

"What is it, your majesty?" they asked.

"Quick—look sharp! Go into every hole
and corner in London, and see if you can find
me something to equal this beautiful thing that
the queen of the country fairies has found;"
and she described the flower to them.

Then she lay down herself, and slept for a
very short time.

Very early next morning, just after sunrise,
her fairies returned and described various

things they had found.   One brought a little piece of " London pride," and said it was grown in London.   Another brought a daisy from Hyde Park, and another brought a snow-white kitten born in London, and so young that it had not lived long enough to get dirty. Some came back empty-handed, for they said all pretty things were brought into the town from the country.

The queen was angry.

" All that is nothing to compare with what I saw last night.   Surely you have not looked among the human beings !   I tell you the form is nothing.   Have you found no lovely child ? I shall go and see myself.   ' If you want a thing done, do it yourself' is a proverb that is true."

The fairies all retired, looking very much disappointed and sad, as they felt their queen was displeased with them.

Now, the queen had of course power to disguise herself as she liked, so she flew out of her palace in the form of a large common blue-bottle fly.   For many hours she buzzed about

town, but found nothing to please her. She
saw many sad sights, that were, however, not
new to her. At last her attention was attracted
to two men leaning over a wall by the river.
One said, " Then how much did you sell your
child for ? "

" I did not sell her, I tell you. I was drunk
at the time I intended to sell her to an old
couple who wanted to adopt a child ; but on
my way I stopped to drink, and I don't remember what I did afterwards."

" What did your wife say about your wish
to sell the girl ? "

" That's just it ! I'm sorry now I took the
child away from her. She was just going off
to the hospital. I meant no harm, but I was
hungry and thirsty, and I thought as my wife
could not take care of Lily, richer people might
do so. I wanted some money badly, too."

" Maybe you dropped the child in here that
night ! " the other man said, as he pointed
into the muddy water under the wall. The
father grew very angry at this, and he gave
him a blow with his fist. They were both

rather drunk; so the queen saw there was going to be a scuffle, and flew away.

"I wonder if that is the husband of the woman who died yesterday? I should not be surprised if he were, for I remember 'Lily' was the child's name. I wonder how old it was? I shall fly in at every house along the road, and see if I can find a child called Lily."

She was now so much interested in thinking of this, that she had quite forgotten that she was looking for a thing to equal the country fairy's treasure.

She flew into many windows all along the Embankment. Into houses belonging to the rich, into houses where poor people lived, into buildings where hundreds were working, and even into the cellars she sometimes crept. At last, in the evening, she saw, in a narrow back street, a woman playing an organ. She had two little girls with her; one was six years old —sickly, pale, and very thin, who ran along the pavement begging of the passers-by. The other was a lovely little girl of three, who, though she looked delicate and sad, was not

Q

thin enough to spoil the beauty of her features and expression. Many people who passed by noticed her, and spoke to the woman. The fairy queen, who still was in the form of a fly, settled unnoticed on the organ, which was playing, " The Last Rose of Summer." Presently, when no one was passing, the woman boxed the little girl's ears.

" There, take that ! " she said. " When those people passed you should have held out your hand as I told you."

The child did not answer, but began to cry.

The woman continued scolding. " Susan does what I tell her, but you, Ann, are naughty and obstinate. You sha'n't have any supper. Do you hear me, Ann ? Do you hear ? Answer your mother, or I'll give you another smack, I will."

" I am not Ann, I'm Lily, and I want to go back to my mother, my dear mother ! " And then she sobbed afresh.

An old gentleman was coming towards them just then, and the woman pushed the child forward on the pavement.

"Now, hold out your hand this time, or I'll—"

She held out her hand, but the man shook his head, and hurried on.

"There! Again you got nothing! I'd box your ears, I would, only I don't want your eyes to look red. Stop crying, now!" and she turned up another dirty street, and called to the other girl to follow.

The fairy let herself be carried into the woman's home—a small room, high up in a house, where many other people lived. The room had but one small window, a pane of which was broken, and let in a little air. There were a man and a boy sitting eating their supper. Both looked well fed, but ragged and dirty.

"Well, what have you got to-day?" he said, as the others entered.

"Oh, nothing but this," and she emptied a bag of coppers on the table. "The fact is, the child you bought the other day for a glass of gin has cost us three times as much as a whole bottle of gin already, and we've made nothing

by her. The folk look at her and admire her
pretty face, but they give far more to Susan,
who knows the way of running after them, and
never leaves off plaguing them till they give
her something."

"Ay, Susan's a good sort!" said the man,
grinning, "and we got her for nothing."

The woman drew her chair to the table, and
began to eat, while the two little girls sat on
the floor near the window, waiting for the
scraps that should remain. The boy appeared
to be their own child, for he got a good share
of the supper.

Now, the fairy thought she would see which
of these two little girls had the kindest heart,
so she flew on the empty plate near Susan ;
but this girl put out her hand and caught the
fly instantly.

"I've got you!" she said. "Now I'll run
a pin through you. It will be fun!"

The boy heard her say this, and came to
look. "Let me see it!" he said.

"No; I sha'n't open my hand, or it will fly
away," Susan answered.

They got a glass and turned it over the fly quite easily; it did not seem to wish to escape.

"Now for a pin!" said Susan; but Lily got up, and stood looking at the fly.

"Please, please don't torment it—it's cruel. Mother says if a fly must be killed, it ought to be done quickly, like this;" and she clapped her little hands together.

The other children only laughed. "Your mother, indeed! Who was she? This is your mother now," they said, pointing to the woman; "and I may do what I like here, so don't you meddle," said the boy, as he went to look for a pin.

The woman, in the meantime, said there was a piece of dry bread left, and Ann might have it, "because," as she remarked to her husband, "the child will lose her looks if she starves. She's hardly eaten anything to-day."

Saying this, she flung the piece to Lily. Susan eyed it as it fell at her feet. Lily picked it up. It was much nicer than the dirty crusts and pieces of fat they had been given before. She was very hungry, and began to bite a tiny piece, whilst Susan watched her. The boy, in the meantime, had brought the pin, and Lily shuddered.

"If you'll give me that piece of bread," whispered Susan, "I promise to stop Bob from pricking the fly."

Lily hesitated a minute—the little piece she'd eaten had been so good, she thought she could not give up the rest; but when she looked at the fly crawling round and round the glass, she said, "Then take it," and she held it out to Susan, who snatched it from her, laughing, and soon gobbled it up.

"Now, then, we'll stick the fly," said Susan, as she turned to the glass again.

"Oh, but you *promised* not to do it !" said Lily, crying with disappointment and indignation.

"Promises are like pie-crusts!" laughed Susan. But just then something shook the glass, and it fell over. Away flew the fairy through the broken pane of glass, out into the air. Bob and Susan were furious, and accused Lily of letting the fly escape in such loud voices, making such a noise, that the woman jumped up and gave each of the girls a hard cuff. She never asked why, or what, but slapped Susan and poor Lily, who had not even raised her voice ; but Bob was the woman's own boy, so she spoilt him. She never even scolded him, but to-day, as always, took his part and scolded the girls.

Lily crept away, and lay down among a little heap of rags on the floor, in the corner of the room, which was all the bed she had. There she lay and cried until late into the night, calling to her mother in whispers, wondering if she could see her again, not knowing that her mother had died in the hospital the day before.

In the meantime, the fairy had flown home. She had seen and heard enough to know Lily's heart was pure and good, and was certainly the child of the poor woman whose husband she had seen that very day by the river. The fairy smiled to herself, saying, " I've not only found the child, but I think it is just as much a treasure as the flower, and certainly much more alive ! "

It was now evening, so, putting off her disguise as a fly, and appearing in her own form again, she flew to the top of St. Paul's, just as the clock struck twelve. The stars were shining brightly, and there was a silvery light over the dome. The country fairy was sitting there already, her wings shining blue and silver as she gently flapped them backwards and forwards in a little impatient way, awaiting her friend.

"I've found it!" exclaimed the London fairy queen, sitting down beside her. "I've found it! And it's more rare than yours, for it's seldom one finds so lovely and good a thing in such wicked and ugly surroundings as I have done. After all, yours is but a flower growing in an innocent garden! No wonder it is not soiled, and can keep its beauty!"

"Gently, dear sister! Show it me first, and then I will see if you're right."

"No, no; go and fetch the flower. We will lay it then near my treasure, the better to compare them."

"I'll do so; but I fear the flower will fade."

"Only a little sooner than it would natur-ally. That reminds me, of course : the beauti-ful thing I've found is human, and will last, therefore, longer than yours," and she smiled.

"Well, we shall see, we shall see," said the other. "I scarcely can think, if it's human and in a town, that it can be anything to com-pare with mine!"

They agreed to meet at the door of the house where Lily lived.

For some time the London fairy flew in and out of the room, waiting for her friend's arrival, and watching the child asleep. When the country fairy appeared, she exclaimed :

"Come in. My treasure looks even more lovely now, but strangely pale. I fear she is ill," she added sadly.

They flew silently and softly into the room. When the country fairy saw the little girl lying in the corner, the moon shining on her soft hair and beautiful face, she exclaimed :

"How fair, how beautiful and good she looks!"

They laid the flower by her side; but scarcely had it touched her than she opened her eyes, and sat up with a start. Stretching her arms out, she clasped the flower next her heart.

"Oh, beautiful! Sweet lily!" she said, and, looking up to the sky, she seemed to see far, far away, beyond the fairies, beyond all earthly things that surrounded her; and, smiling, she called out, "I'm coming, mother! And see, I bring you this flower!" Then, sinking back with closed eyes, she whispered, "Your own little Lily, mother! I come!"

Both the fairies, with their arms twined round each other's necks, stood for a moment admiring her, and then they kissed her; but they knew she was dead.

"It's happier so for her," said the London fairy, "though it's sad for us to lose the treasures we had but just found. See, your flower is drooping; it has faded."

"Yes, dear sister, but your treasure will live in a better land for ever and ever."

The fairy queens kissed each other, and,

promising never to dispute again, they flew back to their homes.

.   .   .   .   .   .

But when the child awoke in heaven, among the pure in heart, there was the Lily too.

THE END.

Printed by Cowan & Co., Limited, Perth.